Ronald C. Williams

Serving God with Style

Unleashing Servant Potential

Foreword by Walter S. Thomas

An Alban Institute Publication

Library of Congress Catalog Card Number 2002104636

ISBN 1-56699-260-5

To a great friend
Dwight Dallas Vailes
May 1, 1957 – December 25, 2001

CONTENTS

Tables

Figures

The church of Jesus Christ has an awesome mission to accomplish. It must bring the measure of salvation to the world and make disciples of men and women everywhere. That has been our charge for over 2,000 years. Yet over these many years the church has had to develop a delivery system for the message, a training program for "the disciples," and a framework for the leaders who are called to carry the torch. The message is not the problem; the systems and the structures are. The question of this millennium is the question of form. How do we package this message? How do leaders perform in this era? What are the undergirding principles that are necessary for effective leadership? The Reverend Dr. Ronald Williams astutely understands this problem and has stepped into the ring as a formidable challenger to this behemoth of a question.

Serving God with Style: Unleashing Servant Potential is a necessary read for all leaders in the body of Christ. It is based on the premise that faith must be the clarion call of ministry. So often ministry becomes "organizational" and not "foundational," but Dr. Williams takes us back to the roots of our calling and the one who affirms our course of action. He asserts that faith is the essential pillar of leadership. As we struggle to find a theology to guide our ministries, he lays out before us what I call *organizational theology*. He helps us understand how God speaks to us when we are serving in the body of Christ. This allows us to reach a new understanding of God because we have seen God through the eyes of a mission, through the eyes of servant service.

Though this work is written for leaders in the church, it is a worthy read for any who have interpreted their role as a servant of God. It offers insights that can change the way we think and process the work we have been assigned. Yet more than anything, it allows us to play to our strengths and to recognize the uniqueness that God has given to each of us. This is never to be understated. We often suffer from feelings of *low spiritual self-esteem*. This work will help all believers to see that God has noted their potential and called them into service so that they might use it. One of the most powerful things that God does for us is to help us understand, and this book seeks to provide that understanding. Each worker, each servant leader can now declare that he or she has been gifted and empowered by God to do a work for God's glory. Such a revelation unleashes servant potential.

As a pastor of a large, inner-city church (7,000 members) with an ever-expanding mission, I know how vital it is to have leaders who understand their calling and who have their leadership grounded in their service to the kingdom. Though we often talk about faith, there are many who fail to link leadership with faith. The Bible declares "without faith it is impossible to please God"; therefore, every leader must understand that what pleases God first is our stance and then our service. If we serve without being grounded in our faith and without a commitment to what it offers us, we may accomplish tasks, but persons will not be blessed at the level that activates faith. It is faith that really dictates service. As the church embraces this truth, we will see major growth in our ability to win the lost and nurture the saved.

I know that this work has been a labor of love. Dr. Williams's dedication to the work of the kingdom and to developing leaders has been something to see. He has helped us transform our church into a real force for the kingdom. The principles he shares here, we have seen work in our setting. Read on and be encouraged. I tell you now that you will see yourself on many of these pages. This book is written to help you embrace the you that God has been developing. When you finish, go forward and unleash your God-given potential.

DR. WALTER S. THOMAS
Pastor, New Psalmist Baptist Church

The Challenge

Speaking to pastors and other congregational leaders, I've become accustomed to laments regarding the 80/20 Rule. The 80/20 Rule suggests that 20 percent of the members of a ministry or any organization accomplish 80 percent of the work. As much as we would like to believe that ministry organizations are somehow exempt from this reality, observations suggest the 80/20 rule is very much a part of church life.

Numerous biblical precepts regarding the value of a strong service-ethic are no guarantee that ministries of any size won't experience shortages of willing, well-prepared servants of Christ. The 80/20 Rule has even caused me to wonder if the intense involvement of Peter, James, and John in the ministry of Jesus was an intentional development of an inner circle or the result of 80/20 in the ranks of the disciples.

Active involvement of congregational members in the development and delivery of ministry is essential for individual spiritual growth, as well as for the health and well-being of the church. Congregational members are vital in both giving and receiving the blessings of ministering to others. One of the biggest challenges church leaders face is the development of creative ways to engage, develop, and send forth congregants in ministry service. Models developed in secular organizations seldom encompass the sensitivity to the spiritual concerns that are essential to congregational life. Ministry organizations deal in

The essence of ministry is the equipping of congregational members so that gifts and talents are released to meet needs.

a different "currency"—the salvation of souls and the nurturing of people in a growing knowledge of the faith. Preparing God's people for the work of service (Eph. 4:12)[1] is where the integration of faith and service comes to life, giving birth to a spiritually healthy congregation and productive ministry. The essence of ministry is the equipping of congregational members so that gifts and talents are released to meet needs.

What Do You Mean, "Servant Resources"?

When I look out on the congregation on Sunday mornings, I see a multitude of needs and a multitude of gifts and talents. I have witnessed the unleashing of servant potential for the past 18 years at the New Psalmist Baptist Church, in Baltimore, Maryland. In my current position as the Minister of Church Transformation— responsible for facilitating change and ministry development—I've become very aware of the importance of the ministry's moniker "Empowering Disciples." The "Empowering Disciples" motto is another way of expressing the goal of increasing the percentages of members who are prepared to contribute to the well-being of the ministry through service.

Strategic preparation of congregational members for the work of ministry expands the pool of people available to execute the ministry's mission. Failure to foster a relationship of reciprocal development between ministry and ministry members or to expand the percentages of active members can cause a ministry to collapse under the demands of the success that is so passionately pursued. Ministry infrastructures sometimes fail to grow proportionately with the ministry demands.

I'm convinced that two problems exist in the quest of ministry leaders to increase the percentages of congregants who are actively engaged in ministry service. First, current approaches aren't always relevant in the relationship between members and the modern church. Society has changed a great deal in the past 20 years. The experiences that people bring to ministry are very different and rapidly changing, but strategies for engaging members in effective ministry service haven't always kept pace with the changing experiences of congregational members. The current age of technological sophistication and informational access means that the pool of prospective ministry workers is very different from those encountered a short time ago. As a result, the service opportunities and the procedures for making them available will be of more value to everyone if they reflect the diverse experiences of all congregational members. Second, there is a lack of common concepts and language to describe the role of congregants in ministry from a systems perspective. I believe the concepts of "servant resources" and "faith-styles" will contribute to the filling of that void.

Congregants prepared for the work of service are important resources for the advancement of ministry. Service is the defining ingredient for effective ministry. People's "service concept"—their personal view of service—is as important to spiritual balance and ministry effectiveness as "self concept," according to psychologists, is to emotional balance. Faith and service are the distinguishing concepts that separate ministry endeavors from those undertaken in secular environments. It wouldn't be uncommon to work in a secular organization and never engage in a company-sponsored conversation about the relationship between faith and service. Such omission in ministry organizations would be unacceptable. Therefore, it is important for ministries to develop language that addresses the uniqueness of ministry. When referring to the development and organization of ministry workers, the term *servant resources* seems to describe more appropriately the needs of ministries. The term *human resources* simply doesn't fit in the context of ministry, yet the need to develop and manage people as a vital resource is still present. The concept of servant resources more accurately captures the essence of ministry work while also providing a framework for a systemic view of congregational involvement. Efforts to develop servant resources have a dual value in a ministry system. First, servants grow in their relationship with Christ and commitment to the mission of the church. Second, the church benefits as the servants work to build the ministry and make disciples of others. The work of the ministry is perpetuated as more servants are given opportunities to contribute to the ministry's success.

The Pathway to
Congregational Productivity

I can safely say that most congregational leaders strive to strengthen the connection between the spiritual growth of individual members and the advancement of the ministry. The ministry organism is only as healthy as its components. A healthier ministry organism leads to a congregation that is increasingly productive in the pursuit of its mission, vision, and goals. A cooperative and mutually beneficial (symbiotic) relationship exists between individual congregants, internal ministry groups, and the ministry organization. Internal ministry groups suffer without the spiritual growth of those who serve on them, and the overall ministry suffers without strong internal ministry groups. Therefore, ministry leaders must effectively devise ways of creating seamless development, development activities that assist individuals to grow spiritually while also helping to improve the effectiveness of groups. This is the essence of the "Servant Resource Faith-Style Model" and the "Servant Resources Faith-Style Inventory" (see chapter 8 and appendices 1, 2, and 3). They provide a multilevel tool that enhances one's awareness of personal patterns of faith and service, as well as providing a tool that will help to develop strong ministry teams.

The basic premise of this model is that faith is the key to one's ability to excel. It is the spiritual enzyme that permeates every activity, enabling believers to achieve what is good and profitable in the sight of God. Since the strength of this gift and the way it is applied varies widely, understanding individual tendencies can be helpful as believers engage in service activities. The more people understand their behavioral tendencies when exercising faith in service endeavors, the more intentional they become. Increasing awareness by utilizing the "Servant Resource Faith-Style Inventory" and understanding the concept of faith-styles will help to enhance ministry effectiveness and facilitate the transformation of faith into productive ministry.

> *It is the spiritual enzyme that permeates every activity, enabling believers to achieve what is good and profitable in the sight of God.*

What to Expect

This book provides readers with a comprehensive understanding of faith-styles and the ways in which the service of congregants and ministry teams can be enhanced through the new understanding. The 13 chapters are divided into three parts and a conclusion. Part 1, "Fundamentals of Service, Faith, and Productivity," includes chapters 1 through 3 and provides an introduction to faith-styles and puts them in a biblical and theological context.

Chapter 1, "Pursuit of Servant Potential," suggests that our individual perceptions of ministry as sacrificial service and the value of sacrificial service in daily life contribute to the manner in which we execute ministry activities. Four elements of sacrificial service are examined in this chapter: activity, creativity, growth, and purpose. A framework is also provided for examining an individual's concept of service. Contributors to individual service-concept are discussed, such as childhood experiences, transgenerational influences, and personality traits. The relationship between faith and service is also analyzed.

Chapter 2, "Faith is the Key," is an overview of the biblical concept of faith and its importance to victorious living. Several scriptures are examined, addressing faith in the life of the believer. Elements of faith are discussed, such as trusting God, believing biblical testimony about God, and viewing faith as a gift from God.

An examination of the relationship between faith and productivity is presented in chapter 3, "The Productive Servant." Productivity is traditionally considered an economic measure that defines the value of output relative to input. Land, labor, and capital are the elements of economic productivity. In the third chapter, the concept of productivity is used as a framework for considering individual productivity from a spiritual perspective. Faith is described as the most important element in the productivity equation. The relationship between faith, service, and productivity is examined in the context of God's calling, God's love, God's will, and good works.

Part 2 of the book, "Everybody Has Style," focuses on describing each faith-style. This section begins in chapter 4, "It Takes Focus," which details the action style of faith and service and discusses the uncompromising commitment to tasks.

Scriptures and examples from service situations are used to illustrate the action faith-style. Issues such as initiating action, disseminating information, providing feedback, submitting to authority, and evaluating processes are examined.

"Do You See What I See?" is the title of chapter 5 in which purpose is described as the "what, why, where, and when" of our daily lives. Faith leads to the realization of vision. Intentionality is discussed as the core of purpose-oriented faith, and mission and method are examined in the context of one's trust in the Lord. The results of finding divine purpose and the influence on faith and success are also examined.

Chapter 6, "Spiritual DNA," reveals the creativity style of faith and service. Aspects of the creativity faith-style are discussed, such as the importance of creating a climate for creative acts of faith, the tendency to lose focus, the purpose of disorder in creating order, the frustration of boundaries, the power of exhortation, and the relationship between perpetual creativity and eternity.

"Being All That You Can Be" is the subject of chapter 7 and contains ideas about the growth faith-style such as nurturing faith, self-fulfilling prophesies, the importance of rest, promoting growth through spiritual enzymes, growth inhibitors, and growing seasons.

Part 3, "Putting Faith-Styles to Work" consists of chapters eight through 12 and provides detailed information about the "Servant Resource Faith-Style Model," giving the knowledge necessary to discover one's individual faith-style and incorporate the new knowledge into ministry service. A comprehensive description of each axis and quadrant of the model is provided.

Chapters 9 through 12 provide all of the information necessary to interpret the results of the "Servant Resource Faith-Style Inventory" accurately. Each chapter addresses the assumptions, common experiences, personality traits, and potential strengths and weaknesses associated with each faith-style. The conclusion, "The Last Word On Faith-Styles," is a summary combined with concluding thoughts. Also included in an appendix are "The Servant Resource Faith-Style Inventory: An Instrument for Determining Individual Faith-Style" and tools to assist in the interpretation of results. To assist in the application of faith-style principles, each chapter concludes with a summary of key concepts and questions to guide individual study or group discussion.

Before You Move Ahead

I've spent many years studying the path to human potential. In undergraduate school at the University of Tampa, Florida, I was so absorbed by the subject that I completed three majors, psychology, social science, and secondary education. Still craving to understand more about the subject, I completed a master's degree at Johns Hopkins University in Baltimore, Maryland, concentrating in human resource development. Many people would have figured out a few things by that point, but I knew that I hadn't. So I engrossed myself once again in the subject by completing a doctoral degree in management and organization at George Washington University in Washington, D.C., with a concentration in organization behavior and development. Combining this with 18 years of practical experience in secular and ministry organizations has let me know that I've still only scratched the surface, so I'm currently enrolled in a Master of Arts in Religion program at the Reformed Theological Seminary in Charlotte, North Carolina. I must admit with a smile that I realize all answers don't spring forth from the halls of academe. The real equation for effectively integrating faith and service is much too complex. I simply enjoy the pursuit of servant potential and believe that faith-styles are an important part of the equation.

To that end, *Serving God With Style: Unleashing Servant Potential* was written to help you find your uniqueness, connect with the uniqueness of others, and develop collective uniqueness in congregational settings. I believe with all my heart that excellence is unleashed when we operate in the truth of our uniqueness. We reach new heights in our efforts to serve when diversity of personality, spiritual gifts, and behavioral tendencies come together in commitment to a common mission. Such heights can be reached only when we serve in the truth of who God has made us to be and respect the truth of who others are, as we work for the advancement of ministry. The truth does indeed have a way of setting us free. Discovering more about ourselves and the people with whom we serve will go a long way to unleashing untapped servant potential in our ministry teams and congregations.

While you read along, I recommend a technique that I refer to is RIPPing through the chapters. The acronym stands for:

Reflecting, Interpreting, Planning, and Practicing. Reflect on what you read. God's voice becomes a lot clearer when we clear the runway of our minds and focus on the one plan that's attempting to land. I have experienced many mental collisions when allowing too many ideas to land at one time. Take the time to think about the ideas that are presented and how they coincide with your past experiences.

Everything has meaning. We may all have slightly different interpretations. Nevertheless, meaning must be applied for experiences to have relevance. Your ability to share the information with others will be enriched and the resulting discourse will be much more valuable when purposeful interpretation occurs. Whether your interpretation is consistent with the meaning that I intended will sometimes be debatable. But what is most important is that the ideas take on meaning that is uniquely yours.

Planning is important as you seek to apply new meaning and understanding to everyday life. I encourage you and others with whom you serve to read the book at the same time. You will reap the best results when you individually and collectively plan specific strategies for utilizing your new knowledge regarding faith-styles. And don't forget to practice what you plan. I know of too many wonderful plans that never make it to implementation.

Finally, my prayer is that you enjoy exploring faith-styles. There are many stories that will be familiar to those who engage in the work of ministry. I encourage you to compare these experiences to your own and join in the discourse regarding the development of servant resources. Empowered servants bring about empowered congregations. Empowered congregations help to fulfill the mission of the church. I'm grateful and very excited about the opportunity to present the "Servant Resource Faith-Style Model" and the "Servant Resource Faith-Style Inventory"[2] as an offering for the advancement of ministry.

PART ONE

Fundamentals of Service, Faith, and Productivity

CHAPTER 1

Pursuit of Servant Potential

I recently conversed with a senior member of my church whom I've watched serve faithfully for many years. She always seems to be involved when there's work to accomplish. On no occasion have I seen her display anything other than the joy of the Lord, whether comforting a lost child or distributing packages to families in need during the holiday season. Her unwavering commitment is inspiring and also a source of curiosity. While I don't doubt that she's driven by a love for Christ, I wanted to hear her express what working for the Lord had come to mean over many years of service.

The dialogue was rich. Her gifts of wisdom and discernment had certainly been refined by many years of ministry and prayer. Despite the richness of the conversation, one of her comments caught my attention and frequently comes to remembrance: "I've been working on the Lord's program for a long time, but I haven't hit my stride just yet. Believe it or not, my best years are in front of me," she said with a smile.

As you may imagine, her comment led me to share in her smile, and even brief laughter. Yet, reflection led me to a very different view of her seemingly casual comment. In her own way, she was telling me that potential to serve isn't defined by age, tenure, or physical capacity. Servant potential is a much deeper, more complex, concept that can only be successfully examined through a Christ-centered lens.

Servant potential is God's infinite capacity to work through the flawed efforts of human participants. We never completely fulfill our potential for service in this life. Our limitations keep that potential somewhere beyond our reach. Potential is that which can be, but has not yet been attained. Divine power is the catalyst that moves every believer toward service consistent with God's will and purpose. Efforts devoid of such power are often impotent and inconsistent with that very will and purpose.

We all have plans for our lives. Think of the people who grow up with dreams of fame and fortune, dreams fueled by a cultural emphasis on material gain. We know countless stories of those who reach material wealth but fail to achieve a sense of divine purpose. Also many people, even the most fervent believers, languish in a feeling of unproductiveness. As a result, people of faith often struggle to find activities in which their gifts and talents can be fully utilized. Those who serve in ministry recognize that drawing forth full servant potential helps bring to reality the greatest ministry potential.

However, the challenge is figuring out how best to build and unleash the full capacity of servant ability, what the financial world calls *capital*.

Since achieving total servant potential is always beyond our reach, the best that we can hope for is to fully realize our quest to be the best that God wants us to be. This contradicts the concept of "self made" men or women. Notions of self-reliance sometimes hinder our efforts to access God's unlimited power and to make progress in our pursuit of full servant potential. Despite scripture's warnings against ultimate self-reliance, we have the tendency to drift into self-deceit regarding our accomplishments. Proverbs 16:3 states clearly that our thoughts shall be established when we commit our works unto the Lord (see also Ps. 138:8, Prov. 19:21, Acts 5:38-39, and Rom. 8:28). More specifically, something very special happens when our thoughts and efforts become consistent with divine purpose. Our service becomes meaningful only when we realize that God's true purpose is for "everyone to be saved and to come to the knowledge of the truth" (1 Tim. 2:4a NRSV). This is a staunch reminder that anything we accomplish is dependent upon our consistency in following God's will. Otherwise, our accomplishments will never be intrinsically satisfying. Potential, or power possibilities, are abundantly present in godly purpose.

Service isn't always easy to render. Voluntary servitude requires inner attitudinal adjustments to external conditions that are often not conducive to service. The basic question is, "What does it take to render service effectively in an imperfect world corrupted by sin?" Rendering effective service requires an acute understanding of how we react to the world around us. A deeper understanding of our interactions with the environment will enable us to consciously manage our efforts to service.

Service as discussed in the Old Testament means simply "to work." Many references may be found to the Hebrew *abodah*, which means "work of any kind"[1] (Exod. 1:14, 1 Chron. 1:9, Neh. 10:32, Ps. 104:14). When this meaning is placed in the context of its New Testament Greek translation, we discover its true biblical depiction of the work of ministry (Rom. 12:1, Heb. 9:1, 6).[2] We may work in ministry as a form of worship, giving our effort as an act of adoration born of the acknowledgement of God's holiness and perfection. Such adoration evokes acts of sacrifice consistent with God's will and purpose.

As we seek to understand the relationship between service and faith, two observations are clear: First, it's difficult for even the most faithful to maintain consistently a posture of unselfish service. We get emotionally "off track" and sometimes miss the benefit and the blessing of service. Second, service has evolved into a concept with the potential to cause inner emotional and spiritual turmoil. Images of servitude as undesirable drudgery with roots in human history come to mind. Putting these images in the context of contemporary ideas about service reveals a recipe for anxiety and a lack of fulfilling the kind of servanthood modeled by Christ.

The Mind of the Servant:
Our "Service-Concept"

Service is focused on the needs of others. Even people who grew up with a healthy attitude regarding service, nurtured by training and guidance from good parents and mentors, may have a service-concept, a view of servanthood that has been negatively influenced. Service is a dirty word for many people because it engenders thoughts of being exploited, unappreciated, and belittled. The negative concept of service may be the result of negative experiences that can often be traced as far back as childhood. Others who have managed to maintain a positive service-concept and have developed their view of service in enjoyable settings may risk compartmentalization, a belief that service is restricted to only certain aspects of life, such as church work.

Our concept of service should be broadened, and the boundaries between service and other activities diminished. This may sound contradictory, but only if we maintain a negative concept of service. Broadening the idea of what's considered service can be a very positive maneuver in our lives if we operate with a healthy service-concept. In its broadest sense, service is creative cooperation with God. This concept removes boundaries that separate activities undertaken as part of "charitable service" or "church work" from other activities. We struggle to achieve balance between work, home responsibilities, and Christian service—failing to realize that Christian service encompasses all areas of life. The defining factors are how we perceive the activity and whether it fits within a healthy service-concept.

In its broadest sense, service is creative cooperation with God.

I came to this realization while preparing to deliver a seminar entitled "Balancing Work, Home, and Christian Service." I knew the room would be filled with people who were anticipating the formula that would bring balance to their crowded lives. I wrestled with the question by examining my personal situation, which I believed wouldn't be too different from the circumstances of those at the seminar. At the time, family responsibilities, full-time secular employment, ministry, and other activities were pressing me to find balance for what seemed to be an overloaded plate.

Then it dawned on me: activities outside of the context of Christ-centered service create the imbalance with which many of us so desperately struggle. Balance is a simple matter of perspective. Work, fatherhood, ministry, coaching Little League— all are Christian service. When we think of service from that perspective, whether we're singing in the choir, taking out the trash, or writing a performance review for an employee, faith in the God who is worthy of our worship is the common thread.

Elements of Worshipful Service

The four elements of service that provide a conceptual framework for servant faith-styles are action, purpose, creativity, and growth. These elements contain the factors present in any service activity, regardless of the setting. The focus may shift as a result of the setting, but all of the elements are present to some degree in everything we do.

For example, we don't usually see washing the dishes as a growth activity. Even if you're a person who is very achievement oriented, the activity isn't one that appears to lend itself to personal growth. However, achievement-oriented people may find themselves trying to continually improve their lathering technique, which represents a growth or development.

Action

Active service initiates progress toward desired results. We define ourselves as productive when we're able to link activities in a way that allows progress to be made. Service effectiveness and productivity can be measured by identifying the various activities that lead to desired results. Many people maintain a "to-do list" of some type. Some of us keep these activity lists on tiny pieces of paper tucked away in our pockets. Others have adopted the more technologically sophisticated alternatives. Regardless of the mode of organizing our activities, we basically order and monitor our accomplishments in units of activity.

Obviously, some people are better at completing routine daily activities. Recall the last meeting you attended and think about the person who presided. How well did she or he follow the agenda? How insistent was he or she about taking action? Was a lot of time spent working on relationship or insisting on action? Answers to these questions may be indicators of the person's propensity for action. Action-oriented people rarely stray from the path of "meeting the next requirement." Anything beyond "putting the next foot in front of the other" is viewed as a useless distraction.

Action-oriented people often amaze me. In my travels as an organizational consultant, I've seen such people save projects, as well as destroy them. The determination to initiate action can be extremely helpful, as well as detrimental. However, action orientation determines a great deal about how a believer exercises faith in Christ. Everything from prayer to mission work is flavored by one's level of commitment to action. Think of prayer in an action-oriented manner. First of all, an action-oriented person rarely goes into prayer without an agenda. To end a conversation with God without expressing every single detail might mean that God somehow wouldn't understand. There's nothing incorrect about this approach to prayer, nor does it mean that the prayer will be any more or less effective. However, a stark contrast can be drawn between that approach and a freer-flowing, spontaneous approach to communion with God. Action-oriented faith, as is action-oriented service, is much more linear in the way it's practiced.

You may have observed action-oriented faith in ministry projects or programs. There are always those who have a propensity for action. They make the telephone calls to remind everyone of the upcoming meeting, volunteer to put together an agenda, or even take on more than they can accomplish because that's the only way they can be sure activity is occurring. A better understanding of faith-styles will help you place service efforts in the framework of a question, "How are my service tendencies realized in the context of my faith in Christ?"

Purpose

Purpose is a goal set up by choice or perceived as desirable. A sense of purpose is absolutely essential to any endeavor. Activities move along aimlessly if there's uncertainty of purpose or commitment. It's not uncommon for purpose to exist that's totally outside the cause of Christ. That's why, as Christians, we sometimes find ourselves tormented by inner turmoil when our environment seems to be governed by causes that are incompatible with our faith. There are definite decisions to be made when we find ourselves in such situations. We can either attempt to advance the cause of Christ in that setting, or remove ourselves. The only way to know which option is in accordance with God's will is through prayer and listening to God's voice.

For the believer, Christ-centered purpose must always overrule any other agenda that may be set forth. That doesn't mean you don't have a commitment to the purpose of your employer, for the Bible instructs that "Whatever you do, work at it with all your heart, as working for the Lord, not for men" (Col. 3:23). Yet a few verses prior it says, "Whatever you do, whether in word or deed, do it all in the name of the Lord Jesus, giving thanks to God the Father through him" (Col. 3:17). The question of "why" always has a singular answer for those who believe—"for the cause of Christ."

The Apostle Paul sets an excellent example of purpose-oriented faith. Before his conversion, Paul's sense of purpose found an outlet in his determination to destroy the church. He described his pre-conversion determination to persecute the followers of Christ as "intense" (Gal. 1:13), a clear indication of commitment to his purpose of stopping the burgeoning movement.

Action and purpose were obvious themes in Paul's life. He continued to demonstrate commitment to action and purpose in post-Damascus-Road activities, as nothing could deter Paul from what he believed to be his life's calling. The description in 2 Corinthians 11:23-28 of his experience while spreading the gospel would have been enough to deter even the most faithful believer. He describes being imprisoned, flogged, stoned, shipwrecked, deprived of food and sleep, naked, attacked by bandits and by his countrymen. Yet, Paul's single-minded focus on purpose wouldn't allow him to decrease his efforts. Even while suffering imprisonment, Paul rejoiced because his predicament enabled him to advance the gospel and accomplish his purpose (Phil. 1:12-18).

This type of commitment to purpose is healthy if constrained and focused by the cause of Christ. It was Paul's undying belief that the one who appeared to him on the Damascus Road was the risen Christ, enabling him to transform an intense tendency to be purpose-driven into a great evangelistic movement. When we follow Paul's lead, the same thing can occur for us.

I know many people who are purpose oriented, yet they often speak of something missing in their lives. I have an acquaintance who speaks passionately about the benefits of her career. She speaks of the money it makes for her organization, the material possessions that it enables her to buy, and the justification for why the cause is noble. But, she admits to often being left empty because of the cyclical nature of the business. Her sense of purpose is firm and intact when the business cycle is on the incline, but waivers tremendously when the cycle is in decline. She often moved from organization to organization in an attempt to catch the next wave of prosperity, or to connect with a more energized company. This proved to be a corporate game of "cat and mouse" with a tremendous downside.

Growth

Growth is an element of service that involves progressive development toward maturity. Such growth is necessary if service is to be fulfilling. God has placed a need and desire to grow inside of us. In generic terms, to stop growing is an indication of stagnation and eventual death. We stop getting physically taller at the end of adolescence, but we don't stop growing or maturing. We have a certain intellectual capacity, but to stop growing intellectually is usually viewed as a negative. The same is true spiritually. We never want to stop growing in our relationship with Christ. To do so would indicate spiritual stagnation and demise.

When I first entered the full-time workforce after undergraduate school, I still had a lot to learn. I sometimes think about where I would be if that job had been the crowning moment of growth and maturity in my career. Growth orientation will drive us toward finding a more excellent way. Growth-oriented servants constantly seek continual improvement.

Sometimes we look down on people who don't have a strong desire to grow. However, we must be careful about imposing our perspectives about growth onto others. I once had a very capable assistant. He had been with the organization for years, so he understood the history behind many decisions. His knowledge and skills often proved helpful, and he demonstrated intellect that could have taken him through college and beyond. Yet, when encouraged to seek advancement through education, he had no interest. This puzzled me until I realized I was imposing my perspectives regarding growth onto my devoted assistant.

While I'll always promote education, I must be mindful that formal education doesn't fit into everyone's growth formula. Some people seek growth in relationships, while others find different pursuits that matter much more to them than formal education. The reality is that a level of education has nothing to do with whether someone has accepted Christ as Savior and Lord.

Growth opportunities help to keep service work interesting. Most of us want to believe that we can improve the way we do things, make more money, or advance to the next level, all of which can be defined as growth. The opportunity to grow can be affirming, regardless of the endeavor. If we don't understand what growth is and how to achieve it, service activity will soon become frustrating.

Have you ever observed someone who reached the dreaded "plateau," believing they have progressed as far as they will ever go? This can be a terrible position, filled with hopelessness, despair, and depression.

Growth avenues must always be included in the design of service opportunities, regardless of position, title, or activity. This is true in service at home, as well as outside the home. One of the fundamental principles in teaching children a positive view of service is allowing a sense of growth to take root. Encouragement is the fuel that feeds the need for growth. All of us as God's servants must have a belief we can grow in our service pursuits. This is difficult to do without positive reinforcement. Even though nothing is more encouraging in a service situation than individual faith in a risen Savior, we generally grow faster when nurtured by human encouragement as well.

Creativity

Creativity is the ability to bring about or give rise to newness. In the strictest sense, only God has the capacity to create. However, since we're made in God's image and carry divine DNA within us, we have the capacity to manipulate all that God created and to bring about what didn't previously exist. Automobiles are human inventions that resulted from putting together a unique combination of materials found in God's creation. We're creative in the sense that we have the capacity to be innovative.

The ability to be creative can greatly contribute to one's ability to render service effectively. Opportunities to render service sometimes occur unexpectedly and bring along a myriad of challenges that call for unconventional approaches. While everyone is born with unique creative capabilities, creativity can also be nurtured in a manner that better enables us to face probable difficulties. People who demonstrate creative tendencies were probably nurtured in environments where they were encouraged to experiment and explore alternative solutions. Mistakes were likely handled as learning opportunities rather than an automatic cause for punishment. These experiences become valuable in service situations. Years of experience have shown me that people who have spent time in environments that nurture creative tendencies are able to manage the enormous uncertainties that exist in contemporary ministry situations.

Many of us are more creative than we realize. Everyday situations present numerous opportunities to be creative. Parenting, for example, is one of the more obvious service-oriented activities demanding creativity. My parents were two of the most creative people on the planet, with the responsibility for nurturing seven children to maturity. They disciplined according to individual personalities, conserved resources, and paid college tuition for each one. Three children in college at the same time will challenge the imaginative capacity of even the most resourceful and productive parent. Even though this was a union of two college-educated breadwinners, many situations emerged when my parents had to use what was available to create what didn't exist. I still believe that my mother was the actual inventor of TV dinners. She wrapped leftovers in aluminum foil and froze them long before I ever saw this creation in supermarkets.

Faith is the engine that drives our actions. Understanding faith styles will help us "tune our engines" more precisely.

Action, purpose, growth, and creativity are fundamental ingredients in any human endeavor. People often demonstrate behaviors indicating dominant tendencies in one of these elemental areas. Even though people may demonstrate behaviors that are consistent with all four areas, one is usually prevalent. Understanding these behaviors in the context of faith provides unique insights into the integration of faith and service. Faith is the engine that drives our actions. Understanding faith styles will help us "tune our engines" more precisely.

The Productivity Equation

Personal productivity depends upon how efficiently action, purpose, growth, and creativity are realized and accomplished. Since we now live in a culture that endorses the value of speed, accomplishing more in shorter periods of time is part of many evaluation procedures. However, we have to acknowledge that there's a quality as well as a quantity consideration when discussing productivity. How miserable would we be if we accomplished a great deal, but the quality of the service and our sense of fulfillment lagged woefully behind?

Some ministry organizations suffer from a lack of concern for personal productivity. Productivity is usually examined from a group or ministry perspective. People are left to make efforts to fit their personal styles into generic formulas for productivity. As a result, those who serve find themselves stressed by the effort to stay ahead of an accelerating, ever-evolving scheme for "getting it done." Leaders and service providers in all types of organizations could benefit from tools that provide a deeper understanding of people. While there are many inventories, assessments, and surveys designed to provide a framework for understanding individual personality traits, something is missing from these secular tools for people of faith.

When I listen to the aphorisms and phrases believers use, the factor in their productivity equation that defies empirical detection is very evident. A phrase such as "The Lord will make a way" may be rendered when difficulties arise. A phrase such as "The Lord will provide" may be offered to address an unforeseen shortage of resources. Phrases such as these are often expressed without real consideration for what they mean in the process of reaching one's goal. These phrases are indicators of an ingredient that's not discussed by theorists in most secular disciplines, or other people who seek to understand the behavioral aspects of achievement.

I believe it's time to re-examine the equations we set forth for personal productivity. It's not that religious thinkers haven't discussed faith; there are innumerable books that are well grounded in scripture on the subject of faith. However, I propose a framework that takes us to a new level of understanding, so we may apply our faith more effectively. The formula for personal productivity will always be debatable. For people of faith, the necessity for faith is undeniable.

Faith Matters

Michael has been the advisor for the Christian student organization for five years. He serves a group comprised of about 10 active members. The numbers usually swell during membership drives at the beginning of each semester and shrink to the faithful 10 before the semester ends. Michael has thought of giving up the advisor's role many times, but something happens to cause him to reconsider every time he attempts to act on this notion. He feels compelled to serve although there's no monetary reward for advisory activity, just the demand for time and work.

What keeps Michael involved? It is his devotion to Christ that fuels his desire to see young people make a commitment to following Christ and becoming empowered by God's Spirit. There's a connection between his faith in Christ, his advisory activity, and God's purpose for his life. If Michael relinquished his involvement with the student group, he would surely be involved in some other ministry-related activity because he's committed to serving God. Yet, he's inspired to stay involved with the students. Michael's deepest motivation seems not to be that the students offer something special, but rather is his discernment of the revelation of God's will and his desire to see God's will occur.

We should strive for our faith in God's ability to provide, guide, protect, instruct, and to override through all, even difficulties. Faith matters in every situation that emerges. We're empowered as servants when we remember that action, purpose, growth, and creativity will be fully realized only when governed by faith in Christ.

Style Points

Style refers to a manner of expressing or accomplishing a desired result, expressing what's inside of us. Generally, everyone has a style that's the culmination of personality, genetics, and beliefs. We "carry ourselves" in a particular way. Others recognize us by our styles. If we think of some of the most influential, memorable people in our lives, we would often recall them because of their style. That was the case with one of my undergraduate psychology professors, Dr. Adams. There was nothing about Dr. Adams' physical appearance that would draw a lot of attention. In fact, he would probably have gone very unnoticed in a crowd. However, there was something very captivating about his teaching style. He is the only person I've ever known who could make a neurophysiological psychology lecture interesting for an hour-and-a-half, two days a week, for an entire semester. His ability to arrest the class's attention had nothing to do with the material; it was his style.

Styles may also be referred to as observable patterns of behavior that are manifestations of who we are mentally and spiritually. Patterns of behavior are observable. Therefore, they represent an excellent way to peer into mental and spiritual conditions that are otherwise subjective and unobservable. We may say that a person possesses faith, but how is the expression of faith manifested in daily activities that reveal individual style? How does my faith influence my ability to accomplish my goals? How do my patterns of behavior that emerge in interactions with others affect my ability to serve with them effectively? These are questions that can be answered through an in-depth examination and dialogue about faith-styles.

Styles aren't to be assessed in an attempt to find a better style. In the context of rendering service, one style of exercising faith isn't better than any other. Styles are assessed purely for the purpose of achieving greater understanding so that we may strengthen our application of faith. The writer of Proverbs admonishes us to "get understanding" (Prov. 4:7). Understanding illuminates God's will and helps us to integrate our personal styles into a more effective collaborative effort for building the kingdom of God.

Our personal styles point the way to a greater understanding of who we are in Christ. Our greater understanding of who we are will lead to a greater relationship with Christ.

Examining our personal faith styles is an essential part of understanding who we are in Christ and how our styles influence our heavenly and earthly relationships.

Relationships are enhanced when people gain greater insight about themselves. My wife and I have been married for twenty years. My relationship with her strengthened as I discovered more about myself. Understanding myself has enabled me not to be deceived and trapped by personal tendencies that aren't conducive to a healthy relationship. Leaving the kitchen in a mess may be a tendency that was already developed by the time I married. Yet, it would be inconsiderate not to re-evaluate my habits in the context of the marriage, especially considering that a messy kitchen may go against the personal tendencies of my spouse. I should therefore examine my preferences and assess how they influence the relationship.

The same is true when we're in Christ. We have to examine our tendencies and determine how they influence our relationship with our spiritual partners, as well as those with whom we are in earthly relationship. Examining our personal faith styles is an essential part of understanding who we are in Christ and how our styles influence our heavenly and earthly relationships.

Summary

Service is so much a part of faith-based endeavors that understanding more about faith in the context of these activities will liberate us in other areas of our lives. In the Christian context, work amounts to service. All honest and beneficial activity has the potential of being Christian service, whether at home, our place of employment, or church. That's why the examination of faith-styles is so important to our total existence, not just to our church life.

Action, purpose, growth, and creativity are elements of service to which we can easily relate. We can observe their value in everything we do. Because the believer possesses faith in Christ as a driving force, all aspects of service must be seen in this context. The faith factor enables us to be more productive in God's sight. Earthly measures of productivity are dominated by the acquisition of material possessions and wealth. Spiritual measures of productivity are gauged by the strength of our union with the divine nature of Christ. This union can only be strengthened by faith. No other catalyst will advance spiritual productivity, and it's impossible to please God without it (Heb. 11:6).

Discussion Guide

1. Do you perceive a difference between spiritual productivity and productivity in other areas of your life?

2. In your current service efforts, are there situations that are difficult because of conflicting styles? What are they? What has been the result of the situations?

3. Do you believe that you can alter your style(s) to become more effective in your service efforts? If so, explain how and why.

4. Are you involved in the type of service you believe God has called you to perform? Are you moving in that direction?

5. What impact do you believe fulfilling your calling will have on the way you exercise faith?

CHAPTER 2

Faith Is the Key

Michelle Akers appeared in a *Today* show interview on July 13, 1999, three days after the U. S. Women's Soccer Team defeated the Chinese team in the Women's World Cup Finals. Katie Couric spoke of her heroic efforts during the exciting victory. Michelle's contribution was recognized as even more phenomenal considering her battle with Chronic Fatigue and Immune Dysfunction Syndrome (CFIDS), a disease known for prolonged debilitation, fatigue, and a multitude of nonspecific symptoms. When questioned about how she was able to endure the grueling contest, her response struck me as a perfect example of the extraordinary power of faith.

"I owe my accomplishments to the best care medical science has to offer, and ultimately my faith is most important," she replied. "If my only motivation was soccer, I would have quit a long time ago."

Intrigued by Michelle's uninhibited acknowledgement of her faith as the most important ingredient in her ability to achieve beyond expectation, I visited her Web site and was inspired by her testimony and confession of faith in Christ. Her faith is the basis for everything she accomplishes, and the anchor of her ability to excel.

Ministry leaders continually search for new ways to enhance the productivity of themselves and others who are called to be servant resources for Christ. A demand to do more exists because we have the capacity to do more and a culture that values more as superior. Those who advocate "more as better" may not understand that increasing uncertainty is directly proportional to accelerating change. The faster we move, the more we achieve in a given time period. The more we achieve, the more we live with uncertainties. And the number of responses to uncertainty is limited.

At the two opposite extremes are fear and faith. Fear has more potential to cause us not to act, and not move forward or else to act in un-Christ-like ways. Therefore, it's extremely helpful to manage the way we exercise faith. Faith is essential. Yet, we struggle to explain how to exercise it more effectively.

Lack of dialogue about how to proficiently exercise faith has resulted in unbalanced lives for many because faith is conspicuously weak or absent from certain areas of our lives. Consequently, our ability to "get things done" suffers. For example, imbalance of faith is one reason why some people are effective in their careers and not their relationships. A faith deficiency often occurs wherever ineffectiveness exists. Personal productivity and effectiveness require a catalyst that permeates every activity in a person's life. Since we all exercise faith differently, a greater understanding of personal productivity and effectiveness in the context of Christian faith becomes increasingly important.

Insight into our personal tendencies can be helpful when we begin to lose productive balance. Disorientation, brought on by the inability to reconcile our values and beliefs with what we observe, causes loss of productive balance. It's like putting on a pair of glasses that belong to someone else, resulting in the messages received by the brain to be unfamiliar, distorted, and inconsistent with the ability to transmit visual images. Likewise, a spiritual disorientation occurs when we don't have a clear, focused understanding of how we exercise faith. Our observations, the interpretation of what we observe, and the resulting decisions are distorted. Our actions become inappropriate, exaggerated, or woefully inadequate because we have no real understanding of our natural tendencies. Farsightedness can't be

The more people understand about their behavioral inclinations when dealing with uncertainties, the more effective they can be in using this information to glorify God in word and deed.

corrected by a prescription that's appropriate for nearsightedness. Those who demonstrate a dominant proclivity toward action in exercising faith will be much more productive if they recognize this tendency and make necessary adjustments for their specific disposition.

The more people understand about their behavioral tendencies when exercising faith, the more focused they become. The more people understand about their behavioral inclinations when dealing with uncertainties, the more effective they can be in using this information to glorify God in word and deed.

Elements of Faith

Even an uninformed nonbeliever may correctly speculate that the Bible addresses the subject of faith. Not beginning our journey there would be the equivalent of starting construction on the world's most beautiful structure without a blueprint or with no foundation. Faith must always be grounded in something. Romans 10:17 tells us that "faith comes from hearing the message, and the message is heard through the word of Christ" (also see Matt. 7:24-27, Luke 6:46-49, Acts 26:16-18, Rom. 9:33, Eph. 3:12). Therefore, the biblical concept of faith must be understood before it can effectively be applied to any aspect of life, including Christian service.

The biblical concept of faith can be defined as a trust or belief in who God is, what God does, and what the gift of faith is as described in scripture. Sometimes we confuse ourselves by making this idea more complicated than it really is. We also run the risk of placing the gospel out of reach for nonbelievers because we speak of faith in terms that seem so unachievable. Jesus provided us with an excellent illustration of the simple nature of faith in the healing of the daughter of the synagogue ruler, Jairus (Mark 5:22-24, 35-43). Jesus responded to the news of the young girl's death in a puzzling manner. Mark 5:36b says, "Jesus told the synagogue ruler, 'Don't be afraid; just believe.'" In his classic manner, Jesus didn't give a long list of spiritual prescriptions, draw upon a theoretical understanding of grief counseling, or use the clichés that are so often rendered in our attempts to soften the impact of devastating news. He simply said, "Be not afraid; only believe."

My interpretation of his response can be summarized by another simplification. There are only two choices: Either you believe or you don't. We may waiver, and doubt may seep into our minds. But when we reduce the uncertainties of our circumstances down to their most basic elements, the uncertainties require an answer to one simple question, "Do you believe?" More completely said, "Do you trust and believe in who God is, what God does, and what the power of the gift of faith is as described in scripture?"

Why Trust God's Character?

Numerous scriptures address the subject of faith with either direct commentary, instruction, or implicit reference in the story. Scripture defines faith and tells us that faith is absolutely necessary in any attempt to please God (Heb. 11:1, 6). When I think of all of the things I hope for, and realize that I have no idea how to make them a reality, the biblical definition of faith becomes more meaningful. I'm fully aware of tenets of culture and secular ethics that describe the way to "make things happen," such as hard work and a good education. But I'm also acutely aware that these desirable qualities will not produce success in accordance with biblical standards. Many people work hard, yet are never fulfilled, and experience a terrible feeling of emptiness and betrayal when the theories and academic exercises fail to address the deeper issues of life.

I sometimes reflect on my experience as a doctoral student at the George Washington University School of Management and Public Administration in Washington D. C. It took hard work to get there (especially considering that I almost failed the eighth grade), and many of my colleagues placed so much hope in achieving the ultimate in academic accomplishment. Yet, there were just as many stories of frustration, failure, difficult life experiences, and pain that couldn't be addressed by being anointed as "Dr. Know-a-Lot." I witnessed the emotional struggles that resulted from the failure of some candidates to achieve what they believed would "make life easier," or place them a "cut above" the rest. As I made my way through those hallowed halls, observing all that God would have me see, it was there that I felt God's call in a deeper way. I realized that the true essence of life could be captured in the answer to one question, "Do you believe in the character, nature, and gift of God?"

There are more illustrations of God's character in the Bible than I could ever discuss in this short book. So I have to be selective and use scriptures that I believe to be most relevant to the topics of faith, productivity, and style (for some representative scriptural references to the characteristics of God, see Table 1, below). I ask that you pray as you read, beginning this very moment, asking God to reveal the truths that will make you a more effective servant for the advancement of ministry. Every person is shaped by genetics and personal experience. What helps you to become more productive isn't necessarily what's required for someone else. I wouldn't dare suggest that I could write a book that will address everyone's individual needs. That's God's responsibility. My objective is to bring your attention to certain truths as presented in God's Word. God's Spirit will take control from there.

Table 1
Belief in the Character of God

God is self-existent (Exod. 3:13-14)
God is self-sufficient (Ps. 50:1012)
God is eternal (Deut. 33:27)
God is infinite (Jer. 23:24)
God is omnipresent (Ps. 139:7-12)
God is omnipotent (Rev. 19:6)
God is omniscient (Isa. 40:13-14)
God is wise (Prov. 3:19)
God is immutable (Heb. 13:8)
God is sovereign (Is. 46:9-11)
God is incomprehensible (Rom. 11:33)
God is Holy (1 Pet.1:15)
God is righteous and just (Ps. 119:137)
God is true (John 17)
God is faithful (Deut. 7:9)
God is good (Ps. 107:8)
God is merciful (Ps. 103:8-17)
God is gracious (Ps. 111:4)
God is love (Rom. 5:8)
God is spirit (John 4:24)
God is one (Deut. 64-5)
God is a Trinity (2 Cor. 13:14)

Believing that God is omnipresent, omnipotent, and omniscient is essential to faith that's going to make us more effective. Our earthly journey can take us to some out-of-the-way places. However, there's no place we can go to escape God's presence. I experienced the depth of this truth while attending a conference in a remote area of Ontario, Canada, which was extremely beautiful, but remote by any standards. Having grown up in southern West Virginia, I'm familiar with rural areas. However, this region of the north surpassed even the experiences of my rural upbringing. One cold, clear night I saw the aurora borealis, more commonly known as *northern lights*, for the first time in my life. The sky was streaming with lights that seemed to dance in the darkness. As the heavens declared God's glory, I was struck by the overwhelming reality that the same God who is characterized throughout the Bible, the same God who was with me in the hills of West Virginia, as well as the streets of Baltimore and Washington, was also in Ontario. The peace born out of that experience strengthened my faith, and God's presence was extremely comforting. God was there; God could see me; and God's power was incomprehensible.

What was a young man from the hills of West Virginia doing in northern Ontario? How did I come to journey to such a place? I'm still not sure why I went, for there were closer conferences that included similar subject matter. But I felt drawn to attend this one. Perhaps it was just for that singular experience. Real trust will bring us to accept that God's wisdom is never wrong. We may not understand the circumstances in which we find ourselves. We may not like the situations that are a part of our present experience. But God's wisdom, the application of unlimited knowledge, is never incorrect.

Examine the issues in your life that lead to a lack of productivity. In many of them, you will find a lack of trust in the wisdom of God. For example, a ministry assignment that you don't enjoy can lead to waning productivity and the question, "Why do I bother to do this?" Contrarily, a question that reflects trust in God's wisdom is, "Lord, what would you have me accomplish here?" Even though the experience isn't one you would have chosen, in infinite wisdom God has given you the assignment for a purpose. God's wisdom is beyond our comprehension. Even though we may see indicators of divine purpose, God's wisdom or the knowledge behind God's decisions may never be fully understood. The doorway to the benefits of divine wisdom may only be entered by faith.

Discussing faith objectively is difficult. That's why I take the approach of describing patterns of behavior, referred to as *styles*, to describe how believers exercise faith. Faith leads to actions that many would consider illogical, causing the application of faith to seem unpredictable. For example, a nonbeliever would find it difficult to understand why a person of limited financial means would trust the provisions of an unseen God. Faith is a spiritual gift, and "The man without the Spirit does not accept the things that come from the Spirit of God, for they are foolishness to him, and he cannot understand them, because they are spiritually discerned" (1 Cor. 2:14). Faith is a supernatural decision to trust an all-wise God.

Humans naturally seek stability in times of rapid change. The world is changing at such a rapid pace that many people experience the anxiety of being forced along, rather than accepting change. The human family is less than 150 years from a totally agrarian existence. One hundred fifty years compared to the complete expanse of human history is a short time. The emotional impact on us is compounded by what appears to be perpetual acceleration. There's no resting place in sight.

I'm often reminded of how fast the world is changing because I spend a great deal of time with undergraduate college students. These are quite different from the evening graduate students I taught during my earlier years as a teacher. The most significant difference is the shrinking of what I call the "window of reference." It used to be that one could remain relevant for longer periods of time. For example, if I made reference to an invention of the 1940s to a group of 20-year-olds during the 1950s or 1960s, chances are that they would be very familiar with the invention because it would have still been in use. However, 20-year-olds in the new millennium have a much shorter window of reference. There's terminology that was very relevant and in use 10 years ago that's completely obsolete today. The pace of change is accelerating and so is the degree of uncertainty we're required to endure. While my attempt to communicate and remain relevant in such a rapidly changing world can sometimes be frustrating, it makes me acutely appreciative of the fact that "Jesus Christ is the same yesterday and today and forever" (Heb. 13:8). We can fully believe that change is wonderful and technology results from creative acts of innovation and ingenuity. However, we're lost without faith in our immutable God. When we discover capabilities such as cloning, which beg for moral and ethical restraint, it's good to have faith in a God who doesn't change.

Faith takes weight from shoulders that are completely incapable of carrying it. An examination of human history, or biblical history, leads to the conclusion that we don't do well when left to ourselves. A spiritually productive life can only be achieved by yielding to the sovereignty of God. Yielding can only be achieved by faith. Giving way to God's control isn't only wise, it's productive. If you believe that God is ultimately in control of everything, you have to also concede that God can accomplish more than we could ever imagine. Paul makes a beautiful statement regarding God's ability to do more than we could ever think when he says, "Now to him who is able to do immeasurably more than all we ask or imagine, according to his power that is at work within us, to him be glory in the church and in Christ Jesus throughout all generations, forever and ever. Amen" (Eph. 3:20-21).

It makes sense to trust in a God who can do more that we can ask or think. We are comforted by the realization that when hope wanes, the sovereign God of the universe has more in store for us than we can even think to request.

God has demonstrated faithfulness, love, goodness, mercy, and grace—time and time again. Human character can be erratic and inconsistent. We fall short on many days, regardless of our efforts. Yet God's character never changes. Even when we waiver or stray, God is always ready to forgive and accept our apologies. God is always available, always ready to listen, and always patient.

Life can be a difficult teacher, but God is always available to give purpose to the lessons that don't make sense. The more we understand about our particular patterns of behavior when we attempt to access God's promises, the better we will be at positioning ourselves to be blessed. That's a good reason to trust God's character.

Why Believe Biblical Testimony?

All of the biblical testimony and prophecy can be summarized in three statements as declared by a God who cannot lie (see Titus 1:2 and Table 2, p.36): "My Son is coming! My Son came! My Son is coming back!"

Numerous reference materials provide lists of prophecies and their fulfillment in scripture. Despite all of the historical, archeological, and circumstantial evidence that supports what we believe concerning Christ, it still boils down to a question of faith. Do you trust God's character, believe scriptural testimony, and accept the power of God's gift of faith? While it's helpful to be aware of scriptural testimony, it's also beneficial to focus on what the testimony means for us in daily application. The misapplication or lack of application of faith can stifle productivity. The absence of faith will cause our "anchors" to drag the bottom of life's sea, requiring that we reduce productivity just to free ourselves from entanglement.

Faith is the essential ingredient in the life of a follower of Christ. Salvation is only a nice idea unless you believe (see Rom. 10:9). Believing that Jesus arose from the grave positions us to receive the promises of God, including eternal life. It also empowers us to overcome the obstacles, hurts, and disappointments of life, which could otherwise render us hopelessly depressed and able to accomplish little.

Think of all of your experiences that left you with only your faith in Christ to get you beyond the situation. A good friend lost his wife unexpectedly after routine surgery. After hearing how he held her in his arms on their living room sofa while her physical life slipped away, I thought how belief in a living Savior was his only hope for moving beyond this tragedy. Even all the visits we made, the food we cooked for the family, and the cards and flowers we sent, as encouraging and comforting as they may have been, couldn't accomplish what his faith in Christ would achieve. Only trust in God can attain such an incomprehensible peace (see Phil. 4:7).

Even less traumatic situations that we encounter daily possess the potential to render us ineffective. Problems at work, difficulties at home, and financial obligations are routine in contemporary living.

Perhaps your child's report card isn't what you think it should be. Or maybe you inadvertently lock your keys in your car with the motor running. It's often those small, unexpected occurrences, not the catastrophic ones, that put a damper on a day that would otherwise be routine.

One afternoon I received a call from my wife while I was working on my laptop. She and a friend had left the house earlier with our daughter for a late afternoon walk along a nearby trail. I knew something had occurred out of the ordinary as soon as I heard her voice. Our daughter had fallen and suffered what my wife believed to be a broken leg. They were having difficulty getting her into our utility vehicle. As I rushed to the scene, it was necessary for faith to override emotion so that I could remain calm enough to do the right things to help my child. By the time I arrived, my wife and her friend had managed to get my daughter into the car. Her leg was indeed broken. What followed was six weeks of drop-off and pick-up duty, since the school bus didn't accommodate backpack-toting 11-year-olds on crutches. Such experiences aren't uncommon to children or parents. However, believing that the Lord will get you through makes it less stressful. The disagreements about who will leave work and make pickups are minimized. The anxiety over a child in obvious pain is reduced. The reduction in personal and family productivity is mitigated. If Jesus can survive the grave, a broken leg is a "piece of cake!"

Table 2
CertainTestimony:
Prophecy and Fulfillment

Gen. 3:15	Offspring of a woman	Luke. 2:7
Gen. 49:10	A savior from David's seed (Judah' posterity)	Matt. 1:1-3 John 6:14
Deut. 1:15	A prophet	Matt. 28:6
Ps. 16:10	Christ's resurrection	John 19:37
Ps. 22:16	Hands and feet pierced	Matt. 26:60-61
Ps. 27:12	False witnesses accuse him	Luke 24:50-51
Ps. 68:18	Christ's ascention	John 15:23-25
Ps. 69:4	Hated without cause	Heb. 6:20
Ps. 110:4	A priest, like Melchizedek	Matt. 1:18
Isa. 7:14	Born of a virgin	Matt. 4:12-16
Isa. 9:1-2	Ministry in Galilee	Matt. 26:62-63
Isa. 53:7	Silent when accused	John 12:13-14
Zech. 9:9	Christ's triumphant entry	Matt. 26:15
Zech. 11:12	Sold for 30 pieces of silver	Luke 2:4-7
Mic. 5:2	Place of birth	
Luke 12:36	Christ's return	
John 14:3	Christ's return	
John 21:22	Christ's return	

The testimony regarding the ascension of Christ can also be particularly encouraging if it's accepted and used to govern our actions. Our productivity would increase if we constantly reminded ourselves that the One who died for our sins, arose, and ascended to heaven where he lives to make intercession for us (Heb. 7:25). Knowing that Christ constantly petitions on our behalf liberates us to attend to the "business at hand," which is to glorify him in all that we do. He's attending to our concerns regardless of what they are. He's there whether we're serving on the church usher board or in the mall attempting to show patience to a discourteous salesperson. Faith assures us that God will always be there to help us accomplish whatever we need to accomplish.

> *Faith assures us that God will always be there to help us accomplish whatever we need....*

An Eye-Opening Gift

Faith is hope, reliance, and trust in God through unwavering belief that Christ died for the remission of our sins, giving us the right to eternal life and all of the privileges as heirs to God's kingdom. Faith opens our eyes to all the characteristics and testimonies regarding the Lord. Without faith, we would remain blind to the wonders, miracles, and joys of Christ-centered living.

How many times have you said, "If I could only see. . . ." or "If I only knew what was going to happen"? The fact is that we don't know. The only thing that puts "wind in our sails" is faith in a God who is all that scripture claims. Faith enables us to move forward, even when difficulties come our way. Faith lets us know that we can prevail, even in the midst of life's most devastating storms, and enables us to be productive regardless of our circumstances.

Nothing compares with gaining the key to our salvation. I remember receiving the keys to the family vehicle for the first time after acquiring a license to drive. I also recall receiving my own key to the family home. I remember the feeling of liberation and inclusion, a whole new world suddenly available. The ability to venture further than ever before, and the experience of not being confined by prior limitations was empowering. The keys were a gift, a privilege, extended by loving parents. The privilege was certainly not warranted by perfect behavior. The keys came as a result of their graciousness and desire for me to experience all they could make available.

Faith serves the same purpose in God's divine plan and is the key to new experiences in Christ. It opens the way to new relationship with Christ. Faith gives us access to all the promises of God. If we want to experience the fullness of our earthly journey and the empowering certainty of an eternity with our Savior, faith is the key. Just as with the keys to the family automobile, we're not so deserving of the faith keys. We receive the keys as a gift, a privilege that the Lord desires for us to have. God desires that we acknowledge our sins and draw closer. Faith enables that to happen.

Since life is relationship oriented, many of the obstacles we experience concerning personal productivity emerge from relationship experiences—spousal, work, extended family, and friendships. The emotional discomfort experienced in damaged relationships has the potential for being more debilitating than physical ailments. I have known people to become ineffective during divorce or severe losses from which they found it difficult to recover. I have also witnessed declines in productivity that resulted in strained relationships among co-laborers in ministry or between leaders and ministry workers. Adversarial relationships have a negative influence on the productivity of everyone involved.

Faith in Christ has the capacity for breaking the stronghold of strife. When two or more people deadlock in contention, faith in Christ enables one or more of them to take the focus off the imperfections of their colleagues and focus on the perfection of a risen Lord and Savior. I'll use the example of two ministry workers to illustrate my point. For no apparent reason, Sandra often tormented Jane, with sarcasm, condescension, and rudeness. I often intervened when the inevitable arguments occurred. Sometimes I counseled the two young ladies separately, providing an opportunity for both to express their grievances without the presence of the other. During the counseling sessions, I made it clear to Jane that I was observing their interactions and that she shouldn't respond to

Sandra's aggression with more aggression. Jane was unable to heed my request. Her retaliation helped to escalate the contention and ultimately lead to her decision to leave the project. Sandra continued to serve.

I came to the conclusion that Jane found it too risky to believe I would fairly handle Sandra's contentious behavior. Trusting God would have enabled her to remain productive and not fall into the trap of trading insults. The gift of faith keeps us from falling into such nonproductive behavioral patterns. I'm not suggesting that Christians should always quietly accept the insults of others. I do contend that once you've experienced unconditional love and acceptance, retaliation is less urgent. Believing in the gift of faith makes it apparent that the Psalmist was correct in saying, "The LORD is a refuge for the oppressed, a stronghold in times of trouble. Those who know your name will trust in you, for you, LORD, have never forsaken those who seek you" (Ps. 9:9-10).

Summary

The biblical description of faith provides the key to our salvation and close relationship with the Lord. We live during a time in history when the pace of every aspect of life has accelerated. The question is "How do we maintain productivity when there's so much uncertainty?" Uncertainty created by rapid, unforeseen change can potentially "paralyze" us with fear.

Economists define *productivity* as the value of input as compared to the value of output. If we apply this formula to our personal lives, the most valuable question is "What are the inputs that will increase the value of our output?" I believe faith in Christ is the single most important ingredient in the formula of personal productivity, allowing us to overcome obstacles that would otherwise stifle our ability to get things accomplished. Faith is the "bridge" which carries us beyond difficult circumstances to the promises of God.

Speaking objectively about such a subjective concept is difficult. Faith defies objective measurement. The best we can do is to describe behavioral patterns that can be observed as people exercise their trust, hope, and belief in a God who isn't physically observable. The first question that must be asked is, "Do you believe in God's character, biblical testimony, and the gift of faith?" Once belief has been acknowledged, patterns of observable behavior can be identified that will help us understand how we live our faith. Our enhanced understanding of personal tendencies in exercising faith provides a framework for discussion and modification, so we can apply faith behaviors with greater proficiency and results.

God's relationship with each believer is evidence of divine character. God's character becomes alive for us when we examine our lives in the context of biblical testimony. The concepts of faith-based productivity and the "Servant Resource Faith-Style Model and Inventory" (appendices 1 and 2) provide a means of qualifying your faith actions in descriptive terms. They will enable you to better grasp your personal patterns of behavior as they apply to the essential ingredient for pleasing God. Christian service is used to focus the discussion of faith-styles on familiar experiences. However, be mindful that Christian service isn't confined to church work. Christian service is something that believers should engage in throughout the course of each day, whether serving food to the homeless, completing a report for your boss, or feeding the family pet. Regardless of your situation or station in life, the sole aim of any believer is to please God. Pray that God will grant you greater insight into how you might render faith that's pleasing.

Discussion Guide

1. Describe an experience in which your Christian service situation seemed to demand more faith than you knew you possessed. How did you respond? What was the outcome?

2. Describe what you know of God's character from personal experiences in service-related situations (in church, home, or elsewhere).

3. Reviewing the list of God's characteristics included in Table 1 of this chapter (p. 30), which has been the most significant characteristic for you in your recent service experience?

4. Which biblical testimony about Jesus Christ is most encouraging to your faith?

5. Discuss three ways in which the gift of faith has opened your eyes to a truth concerning God.

Chapter 3

The Productive Servant

I have been intrigued since childhood by the question, "Why do people do what they do?" In other words, "What compels human behavior?" The questions often lead into a maze of philosophical discourse and conjecture. Our purpose is better served in this chapter by examining the question and the implications from a biblical perspective. This is the only approach that will lead to Spirit-inspired wisdom, knowledge, and understanding of why people engage in specific activities, particularly as they relate to service that's productive in the sight of God.

Drive and motivation are terms used in secular disciplines to describe the psychological elements that ignite human behavior. Spiritual determiners of behavior move beyond the parameters of the human mind into the realm of God, acknowledging sovereignty. God's sovereignty doesn't nullify our free will. We have the ability to make choices. Therefore, the concepts of drive and motivation have relevance in a theological discussion regarding the nature of human behavior and activity. The *Dictionary of Psychology* by J. P. Chaplin, Ph.D., offers the following definitions for drive and motivation:

- *Drive* is an aroused goal-oriented tendency of an organism based on a change in organic processes. Drives may be generated by deprivation or by noxious conditions that give rise to pain. The behavior associated with drives is directed toward eliminating the deprivation or moving away from the noxious stimuli.

- *Motive* is a state of tension within a person that arouses, maintains, and directs behavior toward a goal.[1] ✓

Neither word is ever mentioned in the Bible. However, Paul captures the essence of the definition when he talks about being "compelled" by the believers in Corinth to "become a fool in glorying" (2 Cor. 12:11 KJV). Having his apostleship questioned by a faction within the church and believing that others didn't defend him with sufficient fervor created an emotional discomfort that drove Paul to extremes in the effort to glorify his Savior. When we accept Christ and begin the process of sanctification, ungodliness begins to take on a state of noxiousness. The Spirit that dwells in us is vexed by activities that don't reflect Christ-centered living, creating emotional discomfort similar to that experienced by Paul. We're then compelled to change what we see, hear, and perceive as inconsistent with the cause of Christ. This passion becomes our impetus for service-oriented kingdom building. A committed follower of Christ has a burning, internal desire to engage in activities that advance the kingdom of God.

Service was defined in chapter 2 as "physical or mental activity that occurs in the context of meeting the needs of others." Understanding the role of faith as an impetus for service will help answer the question of why believers serve in the manner that they do, and how faith acts as the spiritual enzyme that enhances the results of service. Faith also refocuses the definition of service by placing emphasis on Christ-centered purpose, or achieving what's good in the sight of God. When service is examined in the context of faith in Christ, the elements of the secular definition are replaced with spiritual elements. Faith justifies the believer. Good works are inspired by a believer's relationship with Christ, a relationship that's only possible through faith. Good works that are comprised of Christ-centered action, purpose, creativity, and growth will enhance the productivity of the believer.

Understanding the relationship between faith, service, and productivity is sometimes difficult for believers, especially those who are new to the body of Christ, because of the misinterpretation of James 2:26 ("As the body without the spirit is dead, so faith without deeds is dead.") and Romans 3:28 ("For we maintain that a man is justified by faith apart from observing the law"). This chapter will reinforce the idea that there's no contradiction between these two scriptures, and that good works and Christ-centered productivity are a byproduct of faith.

Faith, Service, Productivity: The Labor of Love

Without a lengthy explanation, allow me to simply explain that in Romans 3:28 Paul is discussing justification before God. James, however, is discussing works that are observed by people. As James implies in verse 2:22, faith and action work together. As Paul says in verse 3:28 of Romans, we're "justified [before God] by faith apart from observing the law [of Moses]."

A central question when determining the relationship between faith and service is, "How much do you really love the Lord?" That's a question that can be used to snare even the most committed believer. We're easily trapped by this question because imperfection leaves us vulnerable. There are often inconsistencies between our verbal declaration and our physical demonstration of our love for God; and behaviors are often reflections of the heart. Jesus conveyed this truth to the disciples when preparing them for the end of his earthly ministry. He said to them, "If you love me, you will obey what I command" (John 14:15). Obedience is born out of faith in the Word of God. Our service is an indicator of faith and love.

Service environments are excellent for examining love because the relationships are extremely complex and dynamic. We find ourselves in relationship with all types of people as a result of interacting while serving. Regardless of the type of ministry organization, they're all places where we gather to perform functions that we refer to as service. Even if you're engaged in a home-based ministry, such as care giving to an elderly parent, you still experience relationships in the context of your service. Relationship may be with printers, caterers, banks, or others, but they're still interactions with people in the context of service. The critical question is, "Does your demonstration of love in these relationships reflect a deep love for God?"

Consider this scenario: You're put on trial for loving God. The jurors are people you interact with while serving. The only evidence that they have to consider is the behavior you demonstrate while interacting with them. Could they convict you beyond a reasonable doubt for loving God with your entire heart, your entire soul, and your entire mind, or would the evidence be insufficient? Love for God must be evidenced in our relationships with others.

I'm reminded of an incident that convinced me of the importance of demonstrating faith through love. Martin is a director for a large mission-oriented ministry. He has led a small unit of volunteers for several years. His volunteers are ambitious, dedicated, and highly capable. A significant number of people who hold leadership positions in the ministry once served with Martin. Many of his former workers have also gone on to start successful missionary organizations of their own.

One day, Martin and I went to lunch together, as we often did, and I asked him about the success of his group. I was also curious about whether Martin had aspirations beyond his current position. He expressed a deep concern for those who spent time in his unit. His answer was refreshing: "I start preparing my volunteers to leave the day that they start serving. I ask what their goals are and attempt to give them assignments that will get them there. I even have visioning sessions to help them be more sensitive to God's guidance. I never accept personal recognition when one of my volunteers can benefit from it."

Martin provided evidence of love through unselfish sacrifice. As a result he empowered those for whom he made the sacrifice. Faith is expressed through love (Gal. 5:6).

Love is the best evidence of faith that a Christian can offer, and love is expressed through actions that reflect and replicate the love of Christ. Faith and service should revolve around love, and are elevated to high levels when their object is Christ because Christ is the ultimate demonstrator of all that love can possibly be. I'm sure that those who served with Martin weren't

Love is the best evidence of faith that a Christian can offer; and love is expressed through actions that reflect and replicate the love of Christ.

always model servants, but he taught, guided, and sacrificed for them anyway. Most of them responded favorably to his love, and as a result they experienced the grace of God through Martin's actions.

Acceptance of the promise found in Romans 8:28 helped Martin demonstrate his love for God. When one believes with unshakeable confidence that all things work together for good for all who love God and are called according to God's purposes, any motivation for envy, jealousy, or any other potentially negative emotions fade away. Even if Martin remains in his position until retirement, it will all work for good. Scripture doesn't guarantee that Martin won't have difficulties or that he'll not suffer at times. Rather it promises that God has an "acceptable and perfect will" for his life. What a privilege to be a part of God's divine program!

Called

Do you remember the excitement of being invited to the prom or to the party that everyone wanted to attend? A special feeling of validation occurred because those who had the power to invite included you as a requested guest. Acceptance has a way of diminishing the significance of our faults.

Never receiving acceptance can cause severe psychological damage. Those who have never experienced the warmth of acceptance, rejected from childhood by abusive, uncaring parents, siblings, and peers, now may crave to fill the void of attention with destructive activities. Even with far too many stories that fit this pattern, we find solace in the way such individuals increase the significance given to the unmerited acceptance offered by God. God has extended undeserved acceptance to everyone. We're called to salvation that was bought with the blood of Jesus, and have been invited to participate in God's kingdom and glory. I can't think of a single invitation that can compete with that.

God's call isn't without purpose. We're summoned by God to play a part in redemptive activity. Every believer has a part that involves some activity. Many of us spend our lives attempting to find, understand, and fulfill the purpose that coincides with the will of God. Trying to connect with the purpose behind the call can seem overwhelming at times. The call is the easy part of the experience. The invitation is available to everybody. The tough part begins once it's accepted.

Nothing can prepare the believer to realize this purpose with absolute surety. The call is assured, but connecting with the purpose can be like finding your way through a cornfield maze. One reason is that God will never remove the necessity for faith. Everything must be pursued by faith and with prayer, with acute sensitivity to the Holy Spirit's nudging and the whispers of God's voice. What appears to be a disappointment may be a valuable clue to ultimate destiny. What doesn't feel good may actually be valuable. What is defined as defeat may be the pathway to victory. All must be accepted by faith.

Jesus provides a marvelous illustration of the call, and an unlikely path to victory. What must it have felt like to realize that God called you to die for the sins of an ungrateful, undeserving world? Many of us would have responded by saying, "God, I know you called me, but the rest of the message must have been scrambled in transmission!" What level of faith is required to accept an unpleasant assignment that leads to what many would see as defeat? Yet, believers are often called to do this. Comfort is found in knowing that resurrection, victory over sin and death, can only come by following God's will and fulfilling divine purpose. To place it in a modern context, we may experience unemployment, serve with unpleasant people, be looked over for promotion, and get stuck washing dishes three nights in a row. But all of these experiences may lead to victory. All things do "work together for good for those who love God, who are called according to his purpose" (Rom. 8:28 NRSV).

The call is part of the nexus between faith and faith-driven activity. The summons is essential. It's answered by faith and responded to with action, even if the action involves something more akin to wandering. Wandering can be productive if executed with a sincere desire and yearning to connect with God's purpose. Faith doesn't require sight, but does demand a response. Abraham's faith was made complete by what he did (James 2:21-22). Like someone who can't see physically, if you encounter something that *seems* right, proceed with caution. Use the other senses to compensate for the lack of sight. Listen! The same voice that called you will lead you to your divine destiny.

God's Will

Service must be sustained through energy and effort. If there's any doubt about this, conduct a random survey on any Monday morning asking one question, "Do you really feel like going about your business today?" Emotional and physical fatigue diminishes our ability to apply maximum effort and erodes our drive, making it easier to choose inactivity. This is true regardless of how much we enjoy the service activity. Fatigue and the natural tendency for an object to remain at rest are realities of physics and human existence.

For an understanding of how to overcome human limitations, we must again examine the variables involved in achieving what's good in the sight of God (see Figure 1). Love and faith are again part of the equation. In Paul's first epistle to the church in Thessalonica, he expresses gratitude for the faithfulness and growth of the Thessalonian believers (1 Thess. 1:2-3). He lets them know that he continually prays for their service, the product of their faith. He expresses recognition of their service, which is prompted by love. Faith and love act as fuel, moving believers toward God's will. Faith in Christ and love for Christ motivate us to act, even if we don't feel up to it.

The decision to commit to a life of service can require an enormous amount of preparation to successfully make the transition. When I think about what inspires and motivates committed action, nothing surpasses faith in Christ and love for the Lord. As a believer, I would much rather have participants who pursue excellence, report on time, and get along well with other servants because they love the Lord than for any other reason. This connects the service activity with an eternal destiny, rather than an expectation exclusively focused on earthly reward. Earthly rewards are good; however, Christ taught us to place priority on the kingdom (Matt. 6:33).

We're sustained, nourished, and empowered by submitting to God's will. On one occasion, the disciples thought someone had

Figure 1
Achieving What Is Good in the Sight of God

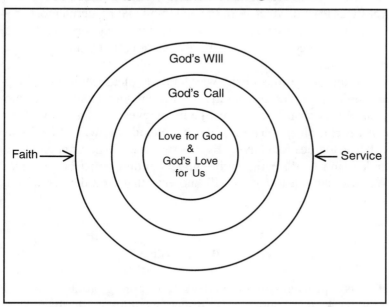

brought Jesus food while they were away (John 4:33). After all, Jesus refused to eat and told them in a direct manner that he had food they knew nothing about. What other conclusion were they to draw? But the Master clarified his comment: "My food . . . is to do the will of him who sent me and to finish his work." His comment made it clear that compliance with the will of God will provide the sustenance, inspiration, motivation, and drive necessary to accomplish what God has given us to do.

Something happens when you commit your life to Christ. I can attest to it, and based on conversations with other followers of Christ, I believe many others will attest to it as well. Since committing my life to Christ, I have been able to accomplish much more with a lot less. It wasn't as if I weren't accomplishing anything before. Many people who viewed my life from the outside would have characterized me as a young "up and comer." The picture was good by most accounts. I was 32 with a wife, two beautiful children, a graduate degree, a managerial position in a world-renowned organization, and I was a published writer, teaching graduate courses for a prestigious academic institution. What else was there to do? Yet I was least productive in the one thing that mattered most, my faith in Christ. As a result, I was running dangerously close to "empty," and could have easily become a casualty alongside the road of life.

If this scenario is in any way familiar, please stop everything and seek God's will for your life. It's the only thing that will sustain you. Money won't do it. Prestige in the eyes of men and women can't accomplish it. There's nothing outside the will of God that will lead to true productivity. Even though we will never completely understand God's will, divine understanding must be pursued. We're to submit to God's will knowing that God desires what's good for us.

Good Works

Here is a problem-solving scenario concerning productivity and good works that I sometimes present at seminars: Martha is Vice President of Community Relations for a major manufacturing firm in an industrial complex in a rural community. She worked hard to achieve her status within the company. Her success is even more satisfying since she's the first in her family to attend college and break into the ranks of professional employment. Her six-figure salary combined with that of her husband, whose career is also flourishing, affords them and their three children a comfortable life-style. The children attend a private Christian school owned by their church denomination. She views all she does as service to the Lord, including her secular career.

Martha's role with the company requires her to have her hand on the pulse of the community. She frequently attends community organization meetings and represents her employer at many community functions, particularly those in which her organization has a direct stake. Her involvement enables her to become acquainted with residents in the community. She attends weddings, birthday parties, and family gatherings during her personal time. This is not a requirement of her employer, but results from her closeness to the community residents and her desire to be a committed servant. Martha is particularly proud of her participation in a mentorship program in the local high school, enabling her to influence young people and help them sort their career aspirations. The president and the CEO of Martha's company are pleased with her commitment to her job and her ability to connect with members of the community.

What seemed to be an ideal situation for Martha was interrupted suddenly. Illnesses began occurring in the community with a frequency that alarmed many residents. Concerns rose about the diagnosis rates of particular types of cancers, as well as an increase in the birth defect statistics among newborns. Martha had heard the concerns before they were expressed officially because of her closeness with the residents. She became aware of research commissioned by her employer to test the toxicity of plant emissions, but had never felt a need to discuss the results since they revealed no health threats to the community. In addition, she hasn't received permission from her employer to make such information available to the public. Martha is also well aware that correcting an emissions problem of this nature would be costly for her employer. When citizens' concerns mounted, the community association commissioned a second study, which rendered inconclusive results.

Martha faces a difficult situation. The people she has grown close to are scared and suffering. She's the voice and face of the organization that residents suspect is responsible for their plight— and contrary to the official company position, Martha believes the plant emissions do present a danger to the community. No other manufacturers in the complex produced anything that could possibly create a problem. Every time she attends a community meeting, or speaks to the media, she wrestles with the notion that she could unknowingly be a part of something that isn't pleasing in the sight of God.

Martha's dilemma is similar to situations faced by many Christians. Potential answers to the problem exist, though none are easy. When I present this situation in seminars, solutions involve: going to the company leaders and attempting to persuade them to change or correct their emission practices, even though their study revealed no problems; sending an anonymous note to the media blowing the whistle on her employer; or leaving the company. There's no easy answer. However, we must remember that what glorifies God may not be easy for us. Martha wants to help maintain the lifestyle of her family. Her children benefit enormously from the private Christian education. If she's perceived as a "whistle blower," she may have difficulty finding another position on her current level. All of these negative scenarios can serve as rationales for not doing what's pleasing to God and consistent with serving Christ.

Good works and righteous work behavior from a Christ-centered perspective can be understood only in the context of motive. The central motive essential in qualifying any activity is love born of a desire to bring glory to God. Jesus instructed us to love our neighbor as we do ourselves (Matt. 19:19), and to love God with all our heart, soul, and mind (Matt. 22:37). Good work emerges from an internal love that finds meaning in its effort to please and glorify God. This doesn't guarantee that all of our work will be good. Nor does it mean that we won't sometimes fall short. However, the desire to glorify God acts as a magnet for our souls, continually tugging on us to repent and return to the path of righteousness. Paul expressed his struggles regarding such matters: "For what I do is not the good I want to do; no, the evil I do not want to do—this I keep on doing" (Rom. 7:19). It's not easy, but good work is always the object of our efforts and the measure of spiritual productivity.

The central motive essential in qualifying any activity is love born of a desire to bring glory to God.

We must also be careful about judging others for what we deem to be good or bad works. Yes, we all have opinions. But, opinions fall somewhere short of judging and condemning. The latter two are God's territory, and Jesus frequently taught the lessons of forgiveness and self-examination. One reason for this caution is that we can observe only behavior, not inner motives. Therefore, our judgments will forever be fallible. On the other hand, God knows our hearts and will be the final judge of all that we do. Just the thought makes me shout, "Thank God for Jesus!" because the reality is that nothing we do is ever perfectly good.

Martha has to pray, and seek God's will in her work situation. This will not be easy, nor will her search for God's will likely be a straight path. God's will is often discovered during the process of searching for it.

Profitable unto People

Profit is the cornerstone of an economic system that has afforded the highest standard of living the world has ever known. Profit results from productivity in which the value of the return exceeds the value of the cost. Profits are then distributed or reinvested to create more wealth and add value. When we think about it, the principles are somewhat the same when explaining faith-based productivity. Salvation renders a return that far outweighs any investment we could ever make. The cost was paid by the only one who could afford it. Yet, look at the return and the distribution of profits. Think about the added value. The profits can only be accessed by faith (Rom. 10:9).

This divine process of allowing believers to take advantage of what God has to offer empowers us in all that we do, giving us access to the same power that raised the object of our faith from the grave. The system of salvation enables us to distribute the benefits of the system to the world through the service we render. As a result, we receive the privilege of participating in what the Bible refers to as *bringing forth*, producing God's will on earth. The words *bring forth* are mentioned numerous times in traditional Bible translations, such as the King James or New King James versions, instead of the term *produce* (Gen. 7:9, Lev. 25:21, Ps. 104:14, Isa. 55:10, Luke 1:31).

Productivity is evident throughout the biblical record. God declared the productivity of the earth by saying, "Let the earth bring forth grass, the herb yielding seed, and the fruit tree yielding fruit after his kind" (Gen. 1:11 KJV). God repeated the process with all forms of living beings. Likewise, the Psalmist says righteous people "shall still bring forth fruit in old age; they shall be fat and flourishing" (Ps. 92:14 KJV). The aim of any productive effort is to bring about what is useful or of service. What we produce is significant only to the extent that it possesses value, or advances our condition. Sin has the potential of corrupting the application of anything we produce, nullifying the profit. There's no guarantee that something won't go wrong in the implementation or the application of what we produce. But better ingredients will produce better results. Our challenge is to integrate faith and service by invoking the love of Christ, adhering to God's call, and submitting to God's will. In that, we will bring forth what's valuable in God's eyes.

The connection among faith, service, productivity, and profit is further illustrated in Jesus' Parable of Talents (Matt. 25:14-28). If we accept the reality that everything belongs to God, then it's not difficult to conclude that we're entrusted with major responsibilities. Faith in Christ suggests that the believer has accepted the responsibility of agency, acting on God's behalf. We believe God empowered us to enhance what was left in our charge. We accept the responsibility of finding a way to use whatever has been supplied us to produce an increase. Even though money was used in the illustration, the principle has broader implications. For example, there was a highly trained physician who graduated at the top of his class from a prestigious academic medical institution. Something happened during his tenure as a medical intern that he didn't anticipate at the time he began his studies: He accepted Christ as his Lord and Savior. Gradually, his priorities were turned upside down. He entered school with the intention of beginning a lucrative specialty practice in a posh suburban area outside the city. Instead, he felt God leading him to one of the less sought-after public hospitals in another metropolitan area. Many of his colleagues, as well as his academic advisor, expressed dismay that he would even consider bypassing the more financially attractive opportunity to practice in such an environment. But he was sure about what God was saying to him: "Take what I'm giving you, and trust me to help you make it better."

Christ-centered productivity is realized when it's rooted in faith. Yes, the young physician sacrificed immediate financial reward. In his words, "I would be less than sincere if I said that money isn't attractive, but I'm in search of a miracle." He took the talents the Master gave him and vowed to produce an increase for the kingdom of God. In doing likewise, we will hear the Master say, "Well done, thou good and faithful servant: thou hast been faithful over a few things, I will make thee ruler over many things: enter thou into the joy of thy lord" (Matt. 25:21 KJV).

Paul explains the relationship among salvation, faith, and good works, and tells how they add value to life: "But when the kindness and love of God our Savior appeared, he saved us not because of righteous things we had done, but because of his mercy. He saved us through the washing of rebirth and renewal by the Holy Spirit, whom he poured out on us generously through Jesus Christ our Savior, so that, having been justified by his grace, we might become heirs having the hope of eternal life. This is a trustworthy saying. And I want you to stress these things, so that those who have trusted in God may be careful to devote themselves to doing what is good. These things are excellent and profitable for everyone" (Titus 3:4-8). Verse eight suggests that the preceding verses can be trusted. That is, we're justified by grace, unmerited favor, and we are heirs to the kingdom of God through the hope of eternal life. Paul stresses this truth so that believers might bring forth good works. The good works of believers will be profitable for everyone. At home, in church, and in personal relationships, we should strive to bring forth what is profitable in the lives of others. "You are the salt of the earth. . . . Let your light shine before men, that they may see your good deeds, and glorify your Father in heaven" (Matt. 5:13,16).

Gathering the Fruits of Faith and Service

The effects of good work are multiplied when individuals come together to accomplish that which is "profitable unto men." There are many congregations across this county, and even around the world, that exemplify effective collaboration in ministry service. One worthy example is New Psalmist Baptist Church in Baltimore, Maryland. New Psalmist has grown from 300 to 7,000 members during the past 27 years under the leadership of Rev. Dr. Walter S. Thomas, who is only the third pastor in the church's 103-year history. If one were to plot the growth curve of the ministry, it would take only a short time to realize that something phenomenal has happened under Dr. Thomas's leadership. Having relocated twice during his tenure, the church has built its newest edifice on a 19-acre parcel located just inside the Baltimore city limits. The ministry also enjoys the benefit of other facilities located on an additional 26 acres in walking distance of the main campus. If there is one characteristic that captures the uniqueness of this vibrant ministry, it is found in the ministry's telltale moniker: Empowering Disciples, which can be translated into "unleashing servant potential." The Empowering Disciples television broadcast, radio broadcast, magazine, and even bottled water are symbols of what is now the hallmark of the ministry, ". . . the perfecting of the saints, for the work of the ministry, for the edifying of the body of Christ" (Eph. 4:12 KJV).

Creating a climate in which those who seek to serve God can reach their maximum servant potential is not always easy, but it is absolutely essential to the well-being of the ministry. The first benefit is that servants grow in their relationship with Christ and commitment to the mission of the church. Second, the church benefits as the servants work to build the ministry and make disciples of others. The work of the ministry is perpetuated as more servants are given opportunities to contribute to the ministry's success.

New Psalmist has certainly evolved over the years. A consistent observation is that those who serve have become increasingly productive as they have been linked together and integrated into the broader mission of the ministry. Linkage and integration cannot occur effectively without tools to facilitate the process. The Servant Resource Faith-Style Model and Inventory are tools that will help you gather the fruits of faith and service.

Summary

Faith-based productivity is the by-product of faith-style efficacy, one's ability to understand and apply faith in a manner that's consistent with one's temperament and personality. We must develop a stronger understanding of what compels us to service for the kingdom. Ignoring underlying motivation and drive leaves us vulnerable. The connection between faith, service, and productivity isn't always obvious. However, the connection is real, and analyzing the connection will lead to greater productive potential. Faith ignites a process that places us in a divine system filled with power that's devoted to accomplishing God's will on earth.

Love remains the essential ingredient in the process of integrating faith and service to achieve a more profitable result. The demonstration of love serves as an indicator of internal motives. The

Faith-based productivity is the by-product of faith-style efficacy, one's ability to understand and apply faith in a manner that's consistent with one's temperament and personality.

power of love that emanates from an internal change possesses the ability to transform the environment in which it operates. The love of Christ must be evident in the life of the believer. How else will the transforming power be released? The evidence of this love must be automatically, as well as consciously, displayed. There are times when it will flow involuntarily because it is resident and alive in us. But there will be other times when the pull of sin will force us to make decisions for righteousness and love. Think of instances when you've had to "catch yourself" and decide to do the Christ-like thing. You may have wanted to lash out in anger, but you decided that demonstrating the love of Christ was more important. Likewise, the impulse to take care of our needs first may be tempting. But the love of Christ is demonstrated through sacrificing for the benefit of others.

God's call to men and women is also central to the process of integrating faith and service. Realizing that God calls us, in spite of our unworthiness, and allows us to participate in divine will is exciting. God's call allows us to connect with purpose that's larger than any personal agenda we could imagine. The purpose doesn't necessarily lead to an easy path or a pleasant experience. The purpose may involve suffering and even physical death. However, spiritual productivity is dependent on one's pursuit of the purpose through acceptance of Christ. Our goal as followers of Jesus is submission to his will and participation in accomplishing God's purpose. Pursuit of God's will nourishes believers, connecting them to God's power.

We're instructed to "let our light shine" (Matt. 5:16) and to be the "salt of the earth" (Matt. 5:13). Believers produce profit that the world wouldn't otherwise receive. The unconditional love of Christ is reflected from our lives for the world to see, so all might come to seek and know redemption. We have connected with God's divine power so we can bring forth what is good and pleasing in God's sight. The salvation we have accepted by faith and received by grace is an impetus for maintaining productive, good works. Faith, service, and productivity are truly connected. Pray that God will enable you to find the connection in your service activities, and serve in a more excellent way.

Discussion Guide

1. What are the challenging conditions in your service experience that you would like to change? How have you tried to change the conditions? What have been the results? What can you do differently to achieve better results?

2. What role does love play in helping you integrate faith into your service experiences?

3. What do you believe is God's purpose for your life? What are the indicators? What are you currently doing to fulfill this purpose?

4. Have you ever been in a situation in which your pursuit of the will of God, in spite of all opposition, gave you strength or power? How do you discern the will of God for your life?

5. How should Martha handle her dilemma concerning the alleged pollution of the community by her employer? (See the section on "Good Works" in the preceding material for the story of Martha, pp. 50-53.)

PART TWO

Everybody Has Style

CHAPTER 4

It Takes Focus

Having prayed for God to use him in new ways, Steve excitedly assumed new responsibility in the media ministry after years of serving in the church bookstore. Monday evening, Steve prepared to attend his first weekly ministry meeting in which members reflect on the Sunday worship and share information about successes, frustrations, and failures. Hank, the media ministry secretary, took pride in setting a weekly agenda that's therapeutic as well as productive for the ministry members.

Steve's role in the ministry up to this point had expanded faster than anticipated. He had developed a reputation for being a no-nonsense person who had a penchant for getting things done. Observing his growth, the pastor believed God had been preparing him for greater work. Even though Steve knew everyone currently serving in the media ministry, this initial meeting represented his first formal introduction into the new role. Everyone arrived on time, and Hank opened with prayer and then asked about each person's weekend. As usual, the question set off a series of stories about family, recreation, and other extraneous activities. Finally, Hank introduced Steve.

The two-hour meeting passed quickly, laced with healthy doses of laughter and brief diversions. Steve observed the proceedings with intense interest and found himself wondering if this was a ministry meeting or social gathering. He felt that too many discussions involved non-ministry related matters. Steve realized future meetings would be difficult for him unless the tempo changed drastically and the "fluff" was eliminated. He would change the meeting procedures as soon as he gained enough familiarity and influence in his new role.

Is Steve correct? Are his new ministry colleagues "slackers?" Or, is Steve just overly serious? These are difficult questions to answer because the culture of every service environment is different. Having fun in service endeavors serves an important purpose, as long as fun and responsibilities are balanced. Meetings also serve an important symbolic, as well as practical purpose. Steve's propensity for action permeates every aspect of his life, including how he exercises faith.

In this book, the concepts of faith, service, and faith-based productivity discussed in part 1 (chapters 1 through 3) provide a foundation for the ensuing discussion of specific faith-styles in part 2 (chapters 4 through 7): action, purpose, creativity, and growth. Part 3 will introduce the Servant Resource Faith-Style Model (chapter 8) and will again examine each faith style in detail, this time through the lens of the model (chapters 9 through 12). We'll begin in chapter 4 by examining the action faith-style.

Initiator's Heart in Action

Getting started is often the most difficult step in accomplishing any task. This is consistent with Sir Isaac Newton's First Law of Motion that asserts, "An object at rest tends to stay at rest unless acted upon by an outside force." I'm reminded of this every time I'm faced with a new or unfamiliar task. The uncertainty and lack of experience means more energy will be required to get started. For many, the required extra energy causes them to remain at rest. On the other hand, initiators are people who often respond to a perceived or actual need with action, seldom waiting to see how others will respond or offer reasons why they're unable to act. Initiators respond in an effort to correct or change existing conditions with faith-inspired action.

Initiators respond in an effort to correct or change existing conditions with faith-inspired action.

Biblical examples of initiative abound. God exemplifies initiative in response to our needs (Phil. 4:19). God's initiatives are always good, righteous, and just. On the other hand, human initiative has the potential for godliness or ungodliness. Consider Isaac's wife Rebekah, the mother of Esau and Jacob, whose life characterized acts of initiative (Genesis 24). When Abraham instructed his servant to go to Mesopotamia and seek a wife for Isaac, Rebekah's initiative served as a sign that she was the young woman God had chosen as Isaac's bride. She also demonstrated initiative upon learning of the servant's mission. Abraham's servant feared that when he found the young woman in accordance with Abraham's specific criteria, she might refuse to return with him. Once again, Rebekah responded with action that affirmed the plan of God.

Rebekah's inclination to respond to situations with action takes on a much different character later in her journey. When the time came for Isaac to give his birthright to Esau, Rebekah once again took action. She willfully conspired with Jacob and tricked Isaac into giving his birthright to Jacob. She felt justified in deceiving her husband because of a single-minded focus on a perceived need of insuring that "the elder shall serve the younger" (Gen. 25:23). Rebekah allowed her zeal for action to manifest as an attempt to bring about what God had already told her would happen. Rebekah's misguided action forced Jacob to flee Esau's wrath. She apparently never saw her beloved son again because she died while Jacob was in Mesopotamia.

When assessing a person's service potential, we normally rank initiative as a positive quality, indicating superior candidacy or merit. However, personal initiative must be examined more carefully to determine if actions are governed by God's wisdom. Long-term productivity is restricted when actions aren't governed by godly wisdom. Even though God's plan was not impeded by Rebekah's deceitful actions, a personal price was paid for her scheming. Those who display an action faith-style must always be sure the end or goal isn't used to justify ungodly means. If we aren't careful, our sincere desire to see God's will come to pass can work against us. As believers, we know the benefits of serving the Lord. We're driven by our love for Christ to work, so all will come to know the Lord. But sometimes our enthusiasm causes us to compromise our convictions.

It's good to have a propensity for action. Such believers pull us from the "ditch of diversion" when we lose sight of where God is taking us. They take action when others idly stand by. But action must always be tempered by God's wisdom.

Table 3
**Activities Associated
with Faith-Inspired Action**

Activity	Definition
Initiation	Beginning an activity or task to achieve a desired result
Dissemination	The sharing of information or knowledge
Filtration	The interpretation of information or feedback based on previous experience and information
Feedback	Receiving information regarding the merit or lack of merit of an activity or task
Submission	Yielding to the desire of someone else
Evaluation	Determining the extent to which a task accomplished a desired result

Dissemination

In the context of service, there's often the need to share information about tasks and associated activities. Much of what we do has ramifications for others. Some of the most intense service-related arguments occur in the home: "You didn't take the garbage to the curb for pick up" or "You didn't take the clean dishes out of the dishwasher." These service-related issues cause destructive conflict. Effective communication helps to minimize frustration and resulting arguments.

Conflict in service environments usually results from unfulfilled expectations. Someone expected a result that either didn't occur or didn't happen in the manner expected. Unfulfilled expectations are manageable, regardless of whether it's an act to be performed or reporting about something that has already occurred. Unfulfilled expectations can never be completely eliminated, but informative exchanges regarding the tasks in question will minimize misunderstandings.

The stories about Moses' leadership serve as a shining example of effective task dissemination. Having received specific instructions from God, Moses disseminated detailed instructions to the Israelite community regarding the tabernacle (Exod. 35-39). He discussed service hours, the building fund, interior decorating, task assignments, materials acquisition, uniforms, and much more. All aspects of the assignments were disseminated in detail. This effective communication was evident in the results. Even though scripture doesn't indicate how often planning sessions or design meetings were held, we can speculate that a project requiring the involvement of over 600,000 people required meticulous coordination and dissemination of information. We can be sure that when it was all over, Moses was pleased because the work had been done exactly as the Lord commanded. The writer of Proverbs is correct: A righteous messenger brings about health and healing (Prov. 13:17).

Action-Packed Anniversary

Church anniversary co-chairs are selected every year. It's always a challenge for four individuals with diverse personalities and styles to develop into a successfully functioning team in just one year. The 1991 co-chairs were long-term members of the growing congregation and had served in numerous capacities, but never with each other. With so much work ahead and so little time to organize, the group was in need of a catalyst.

As her reputation suggested that she would, Evelyn rose to the occasion. An events calendar was developed, subcommittees formed, budgets submitted, and everyone on the committee recognized Evelyn as the "go to" person. As one of the co-chairs observed, "She just has a way of getting things done. She's helped to make this one of the most action-packed anniversary years we've ever had."

Information Filters

Something astounding has occurred over the past thirty years. As discussed in chapter 1, information technology now dominates society. Access and ability to effectively utilize information technology often determines a person's efficiency and effectiveness. The more information technology permeates our daily lives, the more difficult it will become to execute routine tasks, such as shopping or getting a driver's license, without it. The currency of daily activity in modern life is information. The efficient and effective exchange of information influences the growth and productive advancement of participants on the ministry "playing field." The tasks of acquiring and exchanging information demand a great deal of attention.

Activities we engage in while attempting to carry out God's will are always tempered by the information we receive. Action doesn't take place in a vacuum. People act on the basis of the information they receive. The challenge to believers is to manage information and make sure that subsequent action is consistent with the Word of God. Think of the ramifications. It's possible for a well-meaning child of God to take action based on incorrect information.

A member who was obviously anxious to discuss a matter that was causing emotional turmoil approached me one Saturday on the church parking lot. She had just returned from a business trip that involved a week of training. Her company only allowed a modest per diem for food and travel. Not wanting to spend beyond the allowable amount, she asked God to show her a way to eat reasonably well and not exceed the company allotment. Upon arriving at the hotel, she noticed a free buffet offered every evening in the lounge and accepted this as an answer to her prayer. She could now spend more for breakfast and lunch, knowing she would at least have access to the buffet every evening. After several days of enjoying God's provision, another believer approached her as they entered the elevator. The fellow believer cited 1 Thessalonians 5:22 and said, "I've seen you entering the lounge every evening. It doesn't look good for a Christian to be seen entering a bar on a daily basis. I think this is negatively affecting your witness for the Lord." Our member thanked her for sharing her thoughts and said she would consider them. Even though she continued to eat at the lounge, her visits were now overshadowed with anxiety. By the time she reached me, asking if she had done anything wrong, she was in deep despair. She wanted to do what the Lord desired. The information shared by the fellow believer caused great anxiety.

Focus is the issue here. The incident involves two well-meaning believers—one stating that the other's witness may be jeopardized by misinterpreted activity, the other acting upon what she believed to be an answered prayer. The question emerges: "Who is correct under these circumstances?"

The Bible instructs us to "avoid every kind of evil" (1 Thess. 5:22). But in the case just described the verse is taken out of context to condemn an activity that resulted from answered prayer. God knew that the heart of the one who petitioned was asking for provision. First Thessalonians was written to a young church established only a few years prior to Paul's letter that was under pressure of persecution by zealous Jews, angry Greeks, and relentless Romans. Paul's instructions were timely and appropriate for the young believers. However, if entering a hotel lounge to reap the provisions of an answered prayer was sinful, I believe Jesus never would have allowed himself to be in the company of "tax collectors and sinners" (Matt. 9:11).

In fact, the most fertile field for evangelism is among those engaged in destructive behavior. If we're to execute the mission of the church, we will find ourselves among those who don't know Christ. I reminded the troubled servant, "for God is not a God of disorder but of peace" (1 Cor. 14:33). Her motive was pure. The fact that the comments of a well-meaning fellow servant brought confusion and anxiety indicated the advice should have been examined, focusing on what was good (1 Thess. 5:21).

Feedback from the Father

Feedback is more than just a response. Feedback is a reality of our relationship with God, as well as our relationship with humans. Taking action without seeking God's direction will lead to trouble. One role of the Holy Spirit is that of guidance (John 16:13), which implies there's communication and instruction leading to a particular destination. A vital part of any learning process involves practice or application. In chemistry class, we refer to it as *lab*. We can sit forever in Bible study, but if we don't apply what's learned, God's power is never revealed through our actions.

God's guidance is continual in the life of the believer. Jesus promised to always be with us, "even unto the end of the world" (Matt. 28:20 KJV). He instituted a feedback mechanism by which all of our actions can be directed. We're responsible for using the guidance for directing our activities. Adherence to the Spirit's guidance leads to productivity in God's sight. Acts that further the cause of Christ are in accordance with God's will and truth as expressed in the Bible. That's the destiny to which we're led when God's Spirit is operating. John 16:13 submits that ". . . when he, the Spirit of truth, comes, he will guide you into all truth. He will not speak on his own; he will speak only what he hears, and he will tell you what is yet to come."

Faith-inspired action involves endeavors that one believes will lead to a desired result. However, there's often no way to know with certainty that the desired result will occur. I observed action-focused faith in its purest form a few years ago. Don was my colleague, one of God's most devoted servants seeking to serve the Lord in every facet of his life. I watched his professional growth over the years, and his sincerity was evident. Don possessed a strong ability to initiate actions that led to accomplishing particular goals. He had a full-time job as a manager and attended school part-time. The political climate in his organization began to change as the reorganizations of the early 1990s made their way through his company. Since Don was a committed believer, he and I often discussed God's provisions during times of adversity.

One of the changes that resulted from reorganization was the hiring of a new office director, who disliked Don from the start for no apparent reason. Don's work record was impeccable, and he was well liked by the other employees. He continued to interact with the new director in a cordial manner, making every effort to facilitate the director's transition into his new position.

One of Don's projects during this time was to arrange training within a three-month timeframe on a new computer software package for 200 employees. Even with the ambitious deadline, it was perfectly suited for Don's tendency to take action. As part of the preparation, Don felt compelled to include a step that was outside of the normal preparation for such training events. In response to God's guidance, he asked the training department to have each participant sign in for the sessions, rather than following the normal practice of just recording names. Don didn't understand what purpose the signature would serve, but he obeyed the urgings.

The training moved along as planned for two months. One day, Don was requested to meet with the new director and a senior director who worked at the company's home office. No agenda was given, but Don felt the urgings of God's Spirit to take the signatures of the training attendees along with him to the meeting.

When Don arrived, the senior director revealed the meeting's purpose. To Don's surprise, the new director had made accusations that training wasn't occurring. Don sat quietly as the allegations were presented, first by the senior director and then by the director. After they finished, Don presented the actual signatures of all of the trainees who had attended the sessions. The senior director seemed embarrassed, dismissed Don, and expressed a desire to speak with the new director privately.

Conflict and personal vendettas are an unfortunate part of life even as we diligently try to serve and represent the kingdom. Thankfully, God will guide us and give feedback on our activities, as long as we focus on rendering service.

Submitting to God's Authority

Actions aren't often initiated without a desired result because of a belief that the activity will lead to something. However, two realities face servants when faith-inspired action is prevalent. First, even if the tasks are initiated in accordance with God's will, immediate results aren't guaranteed. God's timetable is often different from ours. Likewise, a clear message from God to engage in an activity doesn't mean that we will ever see the results. As difficult as this may be, we must accept our role in God's plan.

How do you think Moses felt when faced with the responsibility of leading the Israelites out of Egypt? He heard directly from God and was set to act in a manner that would bring about the will of God (Exodus 6). He was sure of what God instructed him to do, and yet met with opposition from unlikely places. The first objections came from the Israelites, not Pharaoh. I can only speculate that this was unexpected. After all, he wasn't reporting God's denial of their requests, but God's promise of liberation. Moses repeatedly met with opposition and difficulty. Yet, he took action in accordance with God's direction, believing the desired result would eventually be realized.

Accomplishing what God instructs us to do requires focus, even when opposition slows our progress. Distractions, hurdles, and unforeseen events can be distressing for even the most faithful, but action must be taken. Activity drives the process. We're responsible for taking the appropriate action, leaving results to God's divine wisdom. Remem-bering that results are God's responsibility helps us remain focused on godly purpose. Focusing on tasks at hand also helps us come to terms with the fact that we may never see the results of Spirit-led activities. The action is initiated by faith, and results belong to the One who made the assignment.

Focusing on tasks at hand also helps us come to terms with the fact that we may never see the results of Spirit-led activities.

Any activity that God leads us to is the start of something important. Paul suggested this truth in his first epistle to the Corinthian church. Commenting on his role in relation to that of Apollos, Paul wrote, "I planted the seed, Apollos watered it, but God made it grow. So neither he who plants nor he who waters is anything, but only God, who makes things grow" (1 Cor. 3:6-7). In other words, the one who plants may never see the harvest. Yet he's as important as the one who reaps.

An Old Testament episode also illustrates this principle in a poignant way. Samson's mother, only identified as "the wife of Manoah," was told her son would begin the deliverance of Israel from the Philistines (Judg. 13:2-5). However, deliverance from Philistine oppression wasn't complete until the time of David (2 Sam. 8:1). Even though Samson's part was just a beginning, his actions were important. God's intrinsic authority determines the role we play. Accepting God's prescribed role for us requires total submission to divine authority, which is absolute and unconditional (Ps. 29:10).

Evaluation

A part of Moses' responsibility was to inspect the Israelite community's work (Exod. 39:43). He disseminated the task to the people based on the instructions he received from God. That those who delegate or take responsibility for an act are usually the ones to track the results can be observed in most groups. Groups normally have at least one person who displays the action faith-style and assumes the responsibility for keeping the group moving. This person or persons usually aren't asked to perform this function and may not be the person with positional leadership in the group, but such persons assume the role by virtue of personality and predisposed temperament. If time passes and progress hasn't been reported, the person who possesses the action faith-style will invariably ask for progress reports. If there's any disparity between reported progress and projected progress, this "guardian of progress and accountability" will express concern.

Evaluation is an important component of any productive endeavor. Determining how well we have done enables us to monitor growth and accomplishments. I believe that difficulties arise when the results of an evaluation become known. If a person who has assumed the role or was assigned the role of monitoring or assessing progress determines that the results fall below expectation, then what? This question is critical to the continuing growth and development of those who are being evaluated. Evaluation is essential, but it's not always done in a way that encourages improvement. What's the purpose of evaluating the successful completion of a task? Is the completion of a task the ultimate goal? Or do we, especially as believers, have a responsibility beyond the evaluation event? Do we have a responsibility to assist in positioning the evaluated for another opportunity to succeed?

The importance of this question has become crystal clear, as I have sought to instill a Christ-centered service ethic in my children: "Help the neighbors unload their groceries!" "Go see if the deacons need assistance!" "Shovel the snow from Mrs. O'Connor's steps!" Such words make even the most helpful and obedient children want to take cover. However, these activities aren't just helpful maintenance around the house, but they're also effective for instilling a service ethic and a sense of being a responsible contributor to the well-being of a unit. Children aren't born knowing how to execute these activities; healthy doses of instruction and inspection are required.

Christ-centered evaluation is an opportunity to teach, not punish. Even if the effort is an abysmal failure, the fact that we believe in resurrection implies that life can emerge from the worst of situations. This isn't a matter of letting people off the hook, but pushing and guiding people toward excellence.

The walkway not cleaned to satisfaction means that, as the initiator and monitor of an activity, I may have to coach the young servant through the process of transforming walkways to a standard consistent with Christ-centered excellence. Even though this level of intervention may not be what the young helper would want, it demonstrates a willingness to teach and assist which goes beyond a negative evaluation in the form of yelling and declaring the incompetence of the one being evaluated.

Instruction should never occur without front-end assessment to determine the type and level of instruction required. This sheds new light on Paul's instruction to Timothy regarding teaching (2 Tim. 2:23-26). He told Timothy to be kind, gentle, patient, and courteous in explaining the truth, and to avoid foolish arguments. Evaluations aren't meant to evoke wrath, but to provide an improvement blueprint. If we treat evaluations as opportunities to teach, Paul's words serve us well, and tasks will be accomplished in a greater way to the glory of God.

Summary

Take note of what happens the next time you receive an assignment. Whether you're serving alone or with others, there's a great deal to be learned about how to approach the activity. Some people get started fast; others make progress more slowly. That some people have a more dominant action faith-style than others may create challenges in relationships. It's important to understand how activities are approached and how the approach will determine the outcome.

Misinterpreting deeds or words while accomplishing an activity is easy, inhibiting progress or causing unnecessary anxiety. Therefore, continually seeking feedback from other stakeholders, as well as feedback provided by the Spirit of God, becomes imperative. God has spoken to us through Christ (Heb. 1:2), and continues to speak to us in everything we do.

The outcome of activity is also determined by our willingness to submit to God's guidance. God has a specific role for us that's consistent with divine will. Once we discover our proper role and dedicate ourselves to fulfilling God's purpose, the activities that we engage in will become more gratifying to us and glorifying to God. The glory of God is always our measure of success.

Discussion Guide

1. Do you consider yourself the type that takes initiative easily? How does this help or hinder your attempts to "get things done"?

2. Have you ever received incorrect guidance from another Christian? If so, how did you handle this?

3. What's the most unpleasant activity you've recently undertaken? What steps did you take to help you get through it?

4. What's the best response upon receiving opposition from others when attempting to accomplish what God requires?

5. Think of the last time your ministry was evaluated. Was the appraisal delivered in a Christ-centered manner? Why or why not? What could have been done to improve this process?

CHAPTER 5

Do You See What I See?

I learned a valuable lesson while reading about early seafarers who, because of the inability to see beyond the horizon, rarely left sight of land. Uncertainty about what existed beyond the horizon and fear of being powerless to return to familiar territory kept them from experiencing the excitement of new discoveries. Such is the case with God's purpose for each of us. God's unique purpose for our lives is often far beyond our ability to comprehend or envision. As a result, we cling close to the shore—never experiencing the beauty and splendor of the journey. The ability to move beyond uncertainty is the essence of spiritual growth and maturity. Such ability is a perpetual exercise of transcending the next horizon and exploring unfamiliar territory without the guarantee of a round-trip ticket.

A sense of purpose stands as the most important ingredient in moving beyond familiar experiences. Believers must be irrevocably vested in God's purpose and their role in God's plan. Like the ancient sea travelers, we have no guarantees about what we will encounter in broaching new territory. However, we must be able to see the connection between what lies beyond and our role in God's plan and purpose. God's purpose provides special navigation tools for facilitating the journey. Even in rough waters, purpose steadies the craft. Numerous decisions in my life were driven by a sense of God's purpose, and nothing more. Not only did the decisions require movement into unfamiliar territory, but also traveling in directions that seemed ill advised by other measures. This is purpose-driven faith.

Purposeful faith requires a type of vision that can only be engendered by God's Spirit. The ability to see the relationship of activity to God's ultimate plan and envision outcomes is essential to moving beyond perceived safety. The believer must be able to say with conviction, "I see God's ultimate glory." For example, God might urge you to move beyond your comfort zone with a project requiring hard work, dedication, and earnest prayer. It might be to start a shelter for teen-age mothers, or begin mentoring young males who are getting into difficulty with the legal authorities. It's not hard to see the connection between the shelter or the mentoring and God's purpose. The only question is, "How much more do you envision?" Do you see the mothers being blessed and empowered? Do you see young men being nurtured and fed by the Word of God? Do you see a facility that has all the space and infrastructure necessary to fulfill the mission? Purpose is accompanied by vision.

We can move beyond the shore if we can believe in the possibilities that reside in God's purpose. The vision gives us something to move toward. The vision becomes the radar that enables us to see beyond the horizon, giving us something to strive for. The path isn't always straight, but the sense of purpose and vision keeps us motivated: believing in God's purpose as revealed in scripture, knowing our role in the fulfillment of God's plan, trusting God's ability to take us beyond our limited vision so that we may enjoy a deeper relationship and the fullness of creation.

Scripture challenges us: "Trust in the LORD with all your heart and lean not on your own understanding; in all your ways acknowledge him, and he will make your paths straight" (Prov. 3:5-6). Trusting and believing in God's ability to navigate assures us of guidance. It's not necessary that we always understand, just that we trust the One who is leading us beyond the horizon.

My Father's Business

I once worked with a professor who specialized in matters pertaining to family-owned small businesses, researching and assessing the unique relationships that emerged. One of the most interesting aspects of such business relationships occurs between the business owner and his or her children. Children of entrepreneurs sometimes develop negative views regarding the family business. It's also interesting that third- and fourth-generation family members struggle to retain the business. Succeeding generations don't always share the same zeal, commitment, and purpose of the founders; as a result the family asset is lost.

I think this phenomenon that exists in the secular business world has relevance in our understanding of relationship with God. There's something to gain by asking ourselves whether we're "minding the store." A great deal has been entrusted to us as servants of the Most High. The question is, "How well are we taking care of God's business?"

In John 15, Jesus sets the course and informs the disciples about what's being entrusted to them. He's letting them know that the depth and breadth of his purpose is now being passed on to them. Whatever their agendas may have been, they now must rise to a new level of commitment. He emphasized this point when he said, "I no longer call you servants, because a servant does not know his master's business. Instead, I have called you friends, for everything that I learned from my Father I have made known to you" (John 15:15). Servants have been elevated to the status of friend because of their acceptance of the Master's purpose. Acceptance of purpose is illustrated by actions that are in accordance with the purpose.

Those who accept the purpose of God can be considered privileged. Just as for those who move from the shop floor to the executive suite, there's access to privileged information, resources, and assistance that helps in fulfilling the purpose. All of the love, camaraderie, and friendship that are offered to those who accept God's vision are now available, with nothing held back. Jesus promised his followers that all he

Our challenge is to become better in applying what has been made available by growing in faith and understanding the relationship between divine purpose, mission, and vision.

learned from God will be made known to us, his followers, so that we might effectively contribute to the fulfillment of God's divine purpose. There's no training program on earth that can make the same claim with such surety. We may learn some of the company secrets, but seldom are all of them made available to the apprentice. Our challenge is to become better in applying what has been made available by growing in faith and understanding the relationship between divine purpose, mission, and vision.

Divine purpose has a way of taking our focus beyond the narrow scope of selfish concerns, moving us into realms that transcend the scope of personal interest. This is why the linkage between personal activity and divine purpose is so important. I submit that faith is the strongest link in the connection between our efforts and God's purpose. Without a faith component, the connection between divine purpose, mission, and vision is fragmented and unfocused. When our purpose is driven by faith in Christ, we're engaged in a broader set of priorities. We become part of a kingdom agenda that's always good, perfect, and eternal, but not always understood. Actions based on a kingdom agenda keep us securely in the flow of God's power, which is eternal and never failing. God wants only to trust us with kingdom business and kingdom purpose.

Planning with Purpose

The committee had been meeting regularly for several months in an attempt to complete a comprehensive ministry-wide strategic planning document. Even the efforts of their facilitator to prepare them for a time-intensive, lengthy process seemed to wear off after a while. Some members seemed to lose energy and focus more quickly than others despite any attempts to revive their initial enthusiasm. The original 15-member team experienced attrition that left them with eight regular participants. The remaining eight members seemed to be holding on to something. Their sense of connection between their efforts and the church's mission was evident in their commitment. They exemplified purposeful faith. Their ability to see the relationship between the planning activity and an enhanced ability to serve the Lord made the many all-day planning sessions worthwhile.

Was Paul Serious?

We have come to recognize the Apostle Paul as perhaps the greatest missionary in Christianity's history and also one of the most purposeful characters. He was a product of rigorous training and education, prize graduate of Gamaliel's academy. Paul was destined to fulfill the purpose for which he was prepared. His pre-conversion aspiration consisted of systematically eliminating the movement that would come to be known as *Christianity*. His sense of mission was evident in how he zealously pursued and persecuted the followers of Christ. It would be difficult to convince anyone that Paul was not purposeful, especially the early believers who trembled at the mention of his name. He was serious about his mission and purpose.

What changed as a result of Paul's conversion? His style remained consistent before and after, and the zeal with which he sought to carry out his purpose was the same. Yet, there was a transformation of purpose brought about by an encounter with Christ. I have observed this type of transformation in many converts. Aspects of style, patterns of behavior, and mannerisms remain constant, but there's a totally new focus. An encounter with the divine produces a restructuring of priorities. God uses some of the same qualities that manifested ungodliness to fulfill the heavenly objective for "all men to be saved, and to come to a knowledge of the truth" (1 Timothy 2:4).

Paul's seriousness about God's agenda was born out of a new vision, and his purpose is demonstrated fully throughout all of the epistles. Yet, it's never clearer than when he expresses it in his letter to the church at Colossae (Col. 1:24-29):

> Now I rejoice in what was suffered for you, and I fill up in my flesh what is still lacking in regard to Christ's afflictions, for the sake of his body, which is the church. I have become its servant by the commission God gave me to present to you the word of God in its fullness—the mystery that has been kept hidden for ages and generations, but is now disclosed to the saints. To them God has chosen to make known among the Gentiles the glorious riches of this mystery, which is Christ in you, the hope of glory. We proclaim him, admonishing and teaching everyone with all wisdom, so that we may present everyone perfect in Christ. To this end I labor, struggling with all energy, which so powerfully works in me.

His self-analysis clearly identifies him as a servant who labors with all his energy to fulfill his commission. He's determined to sacrificially put forth his best effort, which is often the case when the Lord reorders priorities. A determination is exhibited that defies earthly understanding. This doesn't suggest that we work ourselves into ill health, as some Christian servants have a tendency to do. It does suggest that the focus of our faith is transformed from the limitations of self to the infinite possibilities encased in godly vision.

We are guided by God's wisdom, which enables us to accomplish divine purpose with increased efficiency. When Paul submitted to the transformational power of God's call, he became a participant in a divine plan that transcended what he knew to be an earthly work bound by the limitations of time. He became a contributor to a divine purpose grounded in eternity.

Something miraculous occurs when we grasp God's vision. We become privy to all the promises offered in God's Word. When style, our God-given tendencies to exhibit certain behavior patterns, is fueled by faith in an infallible Savior, something wonderful takes place. We gain access to what will perpetually sustain us. The fruit of God's Spirit is continuously at our disposal, making it possible to overcome even the most difficult of situations. We're able to sustain focus, maintain hope, share joy, and help to make the gospel real for those who may otherwise be lost. I'm eternally grateful that God allowed me to live long enough to become serious about kingdom matters. Now I can say like Paul, "I consider everything a loss compared to the surpassing greatness of knowing Christ Jesus my Lord. . . ." (Phil. 3:8).

Intentionality

Purpose gives birth to intentions that are the result of placing predetermined values on specific outcomes. In Paul's case, his activity shifted from persecuting to edifying, based on the value he ultimately placed on expanding the movement of the gospel of Jesus Christ. The outcome became his primary concern. Even personal safety became secondary to advancing the cause of Christ. Intention became the telescope through which Paul scouted out his evangelistic quests and became the standard against which he measured the benefit and value of his activities. Only one question was relevant when Paul was faced with uncertainty about his actions, "How will this action produce an outcome that advances the cause of Christ?" I believe that this question led him to boldly declare that he had become all things to all men, that he might by all means save some (1 Cor. 9:22). The important matter is the outcome.

I'm reminded of the power of intentionality every time I interact with the younger of our two children. She's the poster child for purposeful activity. It seems as if she approaches everything with forethought and a specific outcome in mind. Her single-minded determination is evident anytime her focus is challenged by distraction. This is a trait that can sometimes make the parenting responsibility as difficult as it is fulfilling. Trips to the movies are undertaken with extensive planning. School outings are worked out to the smallest detail, even how we will utilize the time during the bus ride. Every detail is envisioned and orchestrated with great precision. And willingly or reluctantly, my wife and I often become participants in purposefully plotted experiences of the daughter we so deeply love. Seldom will we ever be able to complain about the inconsistency of her actions, because what she expresses is most often the path that she relentlessly pursues.

Our daughter's sense of purpose and mission has improved my understanding of ministry, because lack of intentionality sometimes causes frustration in our efforts to serve the Lord. Inconsistency between expressed intent and demonstrated behavior can cause discontent. Simply stated, the problem is that actions aren't always in harmony with words. To accomplish what God has planned for us, consistency must be maintained between intentions, actions, and God's purpose for our lives. Think of the believer who expresses a desire for a closer relationship with Christ, yet never attends Bible study, engages in personal devotions, or gives time in service. Without questioning sincerity, we can certainly say these actions won't lead to the expressed desire.

Numerous reasons can be cited why intention and action may be misaligned, the most obvious being a lack of conviction. The person doesn't really place a great deal of value on the outcome. We have to be careful about jumping to what we perceive as obvious conclusions. Other factors such as emotional trauma or misunderstanding may also lead to misalignment of intent and action. We can't always identify exactly what causes the misalignment, yet we can safely conclude that faith will free us to bring about true alignment. The path God chooses for us isn't always understood, but we must follow the path with all deliberate intention and fervor. There were probably times when Paul questioned whether God really knew best. After all, look at Paul's track record and the hardship he endured. Through it all, faith-driven intentions enabled Paul to accomplish what God desired of him.

Allowing faith to guide our actions isn't always easy, and maintaining focus requires a tremendous amount of self-examination and prayer. Even the most devoted believer can drift into a state of misalignment. We're all subject to the possibility of our activities becoming irrelevant for the winning of souls and the advancing of God's kingdom. Just as we all exhibit different styles when exercising faith, we also have different abilities when it comes to maintaining focus and intentionality. The more purposeful we are in our faith-style, the less difficulty we will have with staying focused. We all have to seek greater understanding of our tendencies in faith matters in order to increase effectiveness. There's more at stake than just wasted time. Our ability to win souls for the kingdom is on the line. As a result, no believer should escape scrutiny when it comes to intent and relevancy. What's our mission? What's the desired outcome? How will our actions help to maintain consistency? Our best intentions are of no value if they fail to bring us closer to the purposes of God.

Pressing toward the Mark

Quick remedies and quick results characterize the age in which we live. The "20- and 30-somethings" have never known an age without advanced technology. While I'm a proponent of the speed and convenience of the information age, I also believe certain realities worthy of reflection must accompany this era. Advances in technology can provide tremendous benefits for the spreading of the gospel,

> *The pressing principle is the unrelenting determination abiding in those who are most purposeful in their application of faith.*

so more people than ever before can be reached with the good news of Jesus Christ. The *pressing principle* is the unrelenting determination abiding in those who are most purposeful in their application of faith. I believe we should examine whether the pressing principle bears as much significance for contemporary believers as it did for the believers of Paul's day. Do contemporary believers have the same determination in the face of adversity?

Believers in Paul's day were totally without the modern conveniences so readily at our disposal. I've heard people say, "I'm grateful to God for the time and place in which I was born." Even though everything isn't perfect, most of us haven't had to endure the persecution and daily struggles faced by believers in the early church. They were under constant surveillance by the religious authorities, as well as the Roman government. Many were forced to stay on the move, meet in secret, and develop elaborate systems of communicating to avoid detection while countering false doctrine and wayward beliefs. This was done at a time when the most basic human needs and concerns were subject to manual fulfillment. Regardless, the pressing principle remained alive by faith in a God who doesn't change.

We all know fellow believers who demonstrate a determination that exceeds the norm, persevering even when faced with overwhelming obstacles. I have a friend who shares a story about his ascendancy to the medical profession. He's a devoted believer and servant of the Lord who fully acknowledges that all he has been able to accomplish is the result of the Lord's favor. A native of the Caribbean, Kenny comes from a family who couldn't afford the expense of medical school. In fact, Kenny was the first family member to venture from their tiny island to pursue higher education. He felt compelled to seek his dream, knowing that it was the call of God to serve others through healing, and to be a witness for God's glory. Kenny felt uncertainty about the source of future tuition, yet he pressed on. Faith and purpose came together, enabling him to continue even when the way appeared impassable. The pressing principle led him to the fulfillment of purpose. Now, Kenny serves his patients with medical proficiency and the encouragement of faith.

The pressing principle shouldn't be abandoned in our quest to serve. Modern technological conveniences aren't just a means of creating a leisurely existence, but afford us more effective methods of fulfilling God's purposes. Purposeful servants are living in the best possible time, with abundant tools available to exercise their unique style of faith.

Perpetual Search

Even the most purposeful believers are on a continuous quest to discover and define purpose. The search is a continual process of interpretations and revelations regarding where we fit in the will of God. It's like trying to put together a puzzle with an inexhaustible number of pieces. You're able to identify progress even while understanding that you will never be finished. The challenge isn't one of becoming discouraged or confused, but remaining determined to make choices that will contribute to the completed picture.

Losing sight of the "big picture" may happen for many reasons. One reality is that God never removes the necessity for faith. We are required to walk by faith and not by sight (2 Cor. 5:7). Sometimes we become overwhelmed by the enormity of what God has called us to do, never realizing we were called to focus on making our unique contribution. I sometimes reflect on the lives of men and women of faith who are recognized for having made significant contributions to the advancement of God's work. We can't allow the advantage of hindsight to overshadow the uncertainties of their daily struggles. This has never been more evident than it was in the life of Rev. Dr. Martin Luther King. Born into a family of clergy, young Dr. King seemed destined for the pulpit. However, I'm certain that there was little in the experiences of his youth that could have prepared him for the enormous contribution that he was destined to make around the world in the arena of social justice. I'm certain that the day-to-day experience of pastoring the Dexter Avenue Baptist Church in Montgomery, Alabama, and co-pastoring the Ebenezer Baptist Church in Atlanta, Georgia, didn't always make sense to him in the scheme of everything else that was happening in his life. In fact, the daily responsibilities of the pastorate, in addition to his national presence as a civil rights leader, probably at times seemed incompatible. Yet, they worked in concert for the purpose God called him to fulfill. He continually discovered his pieces to the puzzle even in the face of great obstacles and the consuming threats to his physical safety.

Purpose supported by faith is characterized by resiliency and the ability to maintain vision, despite overwhelming odds. The search may take you outside your comfort zones, even involving extended periods when progress isn't evident. There may be setbacks that seem impossible to overcome, but the key to successfully negotiating the pitfalls is maintaining priorities and trusting the One who set the mission. The first priority in any search for divine purpose is advancing the kingdom in the hearts and minds of people, not forgetting ourselves. Equally important is the ability to trust God in such a way that we cooperate with divine orchestrations of our journey, believing that "in all things God works for the good of those who love him, who have been called according to his purpose" (Rom. 8:28). The search never ends, but we can rest assured that the benefits are more than worth the effort.

I Feel Good!

Paul's purposeful pattern of service leads to one inevitable conclusion: he was determined to spread the good news and fulfill God's desire of salvation and truth for all people. He sacrificed all that was deemed valuable by secular measures. His accomplishments, education, status, citizenship all took a backseat to his relationship with the Master, taking steps that were considered foolish and treasonous by his Pharisaic colleagues. Yet, he found unimaginable joy in his sacrifice.

People often spend enormous amounts of energy searching for the joy Paul achieved through sacrifice. Frustration arises when the road to joy and contentment doesn't take an expected path or the outcome doesn't yield anticipated results. The key to finding lasting joy is almost too simple to accept. The world has become so complex, accelerated, and chaotic that the simple gospel truth is often overlooked. We're like the inhabitants of Judah during the time of Jeremiah's ministry. The good way where we will find rest for our souls has been made known to us, but we refuse to walk in it (Jer. 6:16). As a result, our joy and strength are exhausted because we attempt to operate outside the flow of divine purpose.

The remedy comes by exercising purposeful faith on two levels of service. First, we must individually search and discover personal purpose as it relates to God's plan of salvation. Second, we must engage in collective pursuit of purpose integrating our efforts into the fabric of others' efforts. Nothing is done in a vacuum.

God orchestrates synergy in the body of Christ even while individual purpose is pursued. Our responsibility rests in finding the stream of common purpose and in remaining open enough to engage others along the way.

This doesn't mean we become irrevocably tied to others. God allows us to engage others strategically in collaboration during a predetermined season. We usually don't know how long the season will last, or know what the result will be, and we find ourselves engaged with others in pursuit of a common purpose, realizing it's only part of God's bigger plan. This truth is amplified in Paul's statement to the believers in Philippi: "make my joy complete by being like-minded, having the same love, being one in spirit and purpose" (Phil. 2:2). The most significant aspect of Paul's comment reveals that his joy is in part dependent upon engaging other believers in collective, purposeful activity for God. He experiences a mysterious sense of satisfaction when he's on one accord with fellow believers in pursuit of kingdom expansion and truth. Joy results in collaborative pursuit of God's desires.

It's practically impossible to experience the joy of the Lord discretely. Others are bound to notice if you've experienced the true joy of the Lord, which leads to another great reality about collaborative service and purpose. A synergy is established when one is collectively engaged in divine purpose. The synergy is born of the encounter with others of faith, which leads to an exponential increase exceeding what we individually contribute. The spirit of disillusionment and doubt can't abide when collective joy, born of collaborative purpose, is prevalent.

The spirit of disillusionment and doubt can't abide when collective joy, born of collaborative purpose, is prevalent.

Who doesn't enjoy being in the presence of people who radiate the joy of the Lord? I look for joy-filled people of faith when I'm having a difficult day. They walk in the climate that repels darkness and reveals purpose so that all may see more clearly and accomplish the purposes of God.

Summary

Purposeful faith is characterized by an ability to transcend the familiar for the sake of fulfilling a higher calling. Trust in God and commitment to God's will enable the believer to venture beyond comfortable circumstances, serving as the catalyst for spiritual growth and learning. Advances, growth, and knowledge of God can't be achieved without venturing beyond routine experiences. Regardless of how anxious we may become, as we learn reliance on God in the midst of our anxiety, we're empowered to connect with purpose and carry out God's will with increasing boldness.

Pursuit of divine purpose is critical for enabling us to care for what God has entrusted to us. We've been blessed with tremendous responsibility to be the "salt of the earth" (Matt. 5:13). We have the task of preparing the bride for the groom's inevitable return. The responsibilities are sometimes viewed too casually. However, purposeful living is dependent upon our ability to recognize and act upon our responsibilities as believers. How much better would the world be if everyone who professed faith in Christ took seriously the responsibility of advancing the knowledge of truth?

Paul is a shining example of someone who took the purpose of Christ seriously. His life-changing encounter with the true and living Christ made an irrevocable impression and transformed him forever. Many came to Christ as a result of an encounter that changed them forever. The circumstances vary, but the impact remains the same—embracing a quest to fulfill God's purpose. Just as in Paul's case, priorities change, and the things that were formerly a priority aren't so important anymore. The only thing that ultimately matters is our understanding of God's will and actively working to live in it.

Therefore, we must continuously assess whether our actions are consistent with the new life that we proclaim. No true believer intentionally deviates from the path of divine purpose. Drifting from the path is the result of succumbing to distractions and temptations that we believe are benign. Nothing in this world is completely inconsequential. We must strive daily to pursue what God has for us. It's easy to get ahead of ourselves by focusing on step three before we get beyond step one. But we must strive to take healthy, effective steps toward God's desire for our lives and the world. The pressing principle is as important today as it was when Paul first described it in Philippians 3:14.

The search for purpose never ends. There's always a higher calling, even when we feel we've connected with God's purpose. God operates progressively, continually moving us higher in grace and relationship. There's danger in believing we have somehow fulfilled God's desires. The best we can express is that we're confident we've put forth our best effort in the attempt. As long as there are people who haven't come into the saving knowledge of Jesus Christ as their Lord and Savior, our work isn't done. If we haven't achieved a church that's without "spot or wrinkle" (Eph. 5:27), there's still work to complete.

So much joy comes in pursuing the purpose of God. There's a sense of satisfaction that assures us we're on the right track. Joy born of godly purpose is an individual, as well as a collective, experience. Think of the joy experienced when we're in the company of like-minded believers, committed in common purpose. Nothing exceeds being in fellowship with those who share the vision and understand the mission of Christ.

Discussion Guide

1. Describe your journey beyond familiar experiences into greater purpose. What were the emotions you experienced during this time? How did you move beyond the emotion into a greater sense of purpose?

2. Explain your responsibility as a steward of divine purpose. What steps need to be taken to make sure you fulfill this responsibility?

3. Discuss the dangers associated with inconsistencies between intentions and actions. What are some areas in your life where such discrepancies exist?

4. Is the pressing principle operative in your life? Give evidence of this principle and discuss how it advances God's kingdom.

5. Discuss your continual search for purpose. Describe how you avoid becoming stagnant in your pursuit.

CHAPTER 6

Spiritual DNA

T he birth of a newborn is one of the most exciting, awe-inspiring events in human experience. My wife and I often reflect on the birth of our two children. Our initiation into the world of parenting occurred in 1983 with the birth of our son. We had been married for about two-and-a-half years, and having experienced one failed pregnancy, we were blessed with the birth of a healthy baby boy. All of the questions and uncertainties gave way to the sounds of crying and 2:00 A.M. feedings. We went from wondering, "Who will he or she look like? What personality traits will emerge? What talents will he or she possess?" to regular trips to the doctor's office and the baby food aisle of the neighborhood grocer. Even while we endured months of anticipation, the answers to many of our questions about the character of our son were resident in our deoxyribonucleic acid, more commonly known as *DNA*, and in the mind of God.

DNA is the substance of genetic markers that determines who we are. Physiologically, we're the culmination of our genetic heritage. God designed a system by which the human species is able to perpetuate and replicate traits that produce uniqueness while simultaneously serving as indicators of family and relationship. The genetic make-up of every person is unique. Yet, there are family traits that are manifested as similarities. We've all heard the expressions that bear witness to our family resemblances: "He looks so much like Uncle Joe," or "She has hair just like grandmother's." Something wonderful happens when two people from distinctly different families, representing distinct genetic heritages, join in a God-ordained union and conceive a child.

A merger of DNA happens in a way that has never occurred before and produces a person who exhibits characteristics from both genetic heritages.

We'll never completely understand how God operates. However, much can be gleaned about the unseen by observing how God has ordered the observable. God has created systemic harmony between heaven and earth, the physical and the spiritual. While the desires of flesh and spirit are often in conflict, we must realize that God designed the systemic movements of both realms, so many parallels exist. The parallels are evident throughout the Bible. While the constraints of time and the mission of this book will not permit me to list all of the parallels and expressions of spirit in the physical world, we should all recognize God's most powerful expression in the person of Jesus Christ. His existence as "the fullness of the Deity lives in bodily form" (Col. 2:9) means that God made the Spirit visible, tangible, and objective so the limitations of our flesh wouldn't prevent us from experiencing the things of heaven. The critical element is our willingness to believe in God's physical manifestation of the divine.

Recognizing the presence of God's spiritual DNA in us is important in understanding who God is and how God operates in our lives. Spiritual DNA was transferred when God breathed the breath of life into man who then became a living being (Gen. 2:7). The first man became alive and took on the character and nature of his creator. The inspiration of God's Spirit that occurred in that breath is the same Spirit that gives us life and energy today. We know that the creation was corrupted by sin. However, the Creator understood the remedy for such contamination. God had to save us through the sacrifice of someone who embodied all that's holy, in order to heal the damage that tarnished the image of holiness. Faith in Christ, the ultimate manifestation of the divine in physical form, repairs the disrupted flow of God's initial inspiration that occurred in the Garden of Eden. Creative faith unleashes the fullness of God's power that resides in us.

In God's Image

One of the greatest parallels between the physical and spiritual in the biblical record is expressed in the creation story "God created man in his own image. . . ." (Gen. 1:27). God, who is spirit (John 4:24), created a physical image and placed it in perfect surroundings. The first humans embodied identifiers that made them an unmistakable product of their spiritual Creator. Our human ancestors' reflection of their Creator also distinguished them from any other creature. Humans are, to our best knowledge, the only being in creation that can relate and consciously commune with God. As the crown of creation, humanity has the rights and responsibilities of relationship with their divine Creator.

Even with the limitations of our flesh and the barriers of sin, knowing that we're made in the image of an infallible, supreme God should influence how we view ourselves. I often think of how parents strive to instill a sense of family pride in their children. I'm sure this practice isn't completely dead. Perhaps, it's not as publicized as some of the less desirable practices that have emerged in family culture. Yet, I remember what it was like to be instructed about how to present oneself as a representative of the family. The concept had more to do with respect for others than the maintenance of false pretenses. The idea was to represent positively those with whom we shared a common heritage, to represent them in a way that upheld higher standards, much in the same way that we strive to maintain a good witness for the Lord.

Another reality is implied in this earthly parallel to our heavenly relationship. When love is the abiding principle in the family, even when the child acts in a way that's not reflective of better virtues, the child is corrected, instructed, and loved to reestablish wholeness and relationship. Unconditional, sacrificial love is the most powerful trait that we inherit from our Creator, which can only be activated by faith. It's contrary to human tendencies and desires for revenge and retribution. This love can only be inspired by our faith in a God who demonstrated power in the plan to save humankind. Numerous traits are found in our spiritual gene pool, but unconditional love has more healing qualities than all.

The demonstration of God's love does more than any one act to illustrate God's character to others. Unconditional love can convert an enemy, grasp the attention of a wayward child, and rehabilitate an addictive personality. Many of us can remember transgressions that wouldn't have made our parents proud. Those that were discovered didn't change their love for us or that we looked like them and bore many of their physical traits and mannerisms. Nothing, no matter how terrible, could change our belonging to them. Such is the case with our Creator. We're part of God's creation regardless of how unworthy we may prove ourselves to be. God's eternal mercy and grace is extended to us as objects of divine love.

As we explore the creative faith-style, we must ask ourselves, "What traits are dominant in our spiritual DNA?" We're made in God's image. God has provided a way for us to overcome the consequences of sin. Therefore, it's incumbent upon us to represent our Creator in the best possible way, allowing the fullness of inspirational power to push us beyond our recognized limitations. The capacity is already resident in us, being released the instant we accepted Christ as our way of reversing the contamination of our spiritual gene pool. We only have to learn to appropriate it in a way that glorifies God in an increasingly excellent way. Faith that inspires enables us to unleash creative capacity and represent the Lord with passion.

My Father's Classroom

Life is one big laboratory for those who exhibit high degrees of creativity in their demonstration of faith. There's no fear of going new places and having new experiences with God. This is faith in a continuous learning mode. I often attempt to explain this concept to the college students with whom I interact on a regular basis. Their tendency to complain about the rigors of college, combined with my

Life is one big laboratory for those who exhibit high degrees of creativity in their demonstration of faith.

personal experiences, caused me to conclude that comfort isn't a prerequisite for learning. I'm referring to physical as well as emotional comfort. I have no scientific data to support this inference, and it's empirical only in the sense that it's based on my observations. However, I'm in many ways convinced that comfort may actually slow down the learning process. Creative faith is perhaps most alive in times of discomfort because of its tendency to inspire believers into new endeavors.

Some of our most creative moments occur when we're under pressure, when "our backs are against a wall." Turmoil is a scriptural guarantee. The Master assured us that in this world, we will have trouble (John 16:33). God didn't say this as a declaration of defeat, but an expression of divine truth. Even with Jesus' assurance that he has overcome the world, he doesn't give exemptions from trouble. Therefore, we must conclude that trouble can serve a divine purpose through lessons learned and a deeper understanding and relationship with God.

Difficulties have a way of bringing about creativity. We have a need or a desire that challenges us. Our lack of resources tests our resolve to continue. A traumatic experience causes us to question our desire to move forward, calling creative capacity into action. While this may seem insurmountable for some, we all know believers who thrive in such situations. It's almost as if they live to be on the edge, and the edge becomes a place of divine inspiration and productivity.

Spiritual growth, like any other learning process, requires a journey into the unknown. Growth is found only in those places and experiences that are unfamiliar. Familiar experiences are referred to as *routine*. Learning and growth is minimized in routine situations. Situations beyond the norm are the playground of those who exhibit dominant creative tendencies born of divine inspiration. Think of the people in your ministry who are always looking to go into uncharted directions, wanting to do things differently. Sometimes their thinking seems to be unorthodox. They seem to have no concern for task, just a passion for experimenting with unproven ideas.

Situations beyond the norm are the playground of those who exhibit dominant creative tendencies born of divine inspiration.

Lack of understanding about creative faith and the way such people interact with other ministry team members can destroy the work of well-meaning ministry volunteers. Those who operate in this manner seldom feel as though they fit in. Those who operate with a great concern for task and purpose often feel as if creative believers are unfocused and "flaky." It's important to understand the roles of various faith-styles in the context of service on ministry teams. Creative believers can be the engines that continuously bring newness to efforts that would otherwise become stagnant and eventually decline. The focus is on learning and growing beyond our recognized capacity, and allowing God continuously to help us break new ground and forge new territories. We must always seek to broaden our potential. Whether the creative spiritual gene is dominant or recessive in our lives isn't the most important matter. It's that we maximize the unique style mix and learn how to interact effectively with others in a way that empowers them to be the best God has called them to be.

Climate Matters

Creative believers thrive in certain emotional and relational climates. That's why it's so important for ministry leaders to have an understanding of the climate type they're creating or allowing to exist. Climate can be a major contributor to servant stagnation and burnout. Environments that are rigid, inflexible, or extremely structured may be comfortable for some and completely stifling for others.

I once worked on a ministry project with a young man named Ramón who was one of the most talented, innovative people I've ever known. He found great joy in applying his organizational skills in ministry projects. If there was a youth program, church fellowship, conference event, or any other project, Ramón proved to be a valuable asset. He had a flair for adding the touch that made the difference between an ordinary and the extraordinary event. His knack for going beyond the boundaries of the expected, combined with his organizational skills made him an active and sought-after member of the ministry team.

I noticed a disturbing situation in a planning meeting for the annual church picnic. The meeting was productive and orderly; the agenda was prepared; the meeting was well attended. However, Ramón seemed distracted, not engaged in the discussion as usual. I thought he might be experiencing personal problems; and, out of concern and friendship, I approached him after the meeting to inquire how things were going, in hopes that I would be able to offer encouragement. His response came as quite a surprise. He wasn't enjoying his participation on the project as much as usual, feeling his contribution wasn't of great value. Ramón wasn't attributing his feelings to the actions of any of the other members. Quite frankly, he didn't know why he felt the way he did. I offered to attend the meetings as an observer and monitor the process to see if I could offer suggestions about how he might get back into the flow of activity.

One revealing observation involved the project leadership. The picnic committee had been under the leadership of one person, Mrs. Tyler, for the previous three years, who was successful in her role with a congenial style. She often started the meetings with a game or icebreaker, and spent time catching up on what was personally happening with each team member. When mistakes were made, Mrs. Tyler always made sure the responsible party understood that some mistakes were a part of every process. Work was accomplished. However, Mrs. Tyler never seemed to take a direct path to achieving the objective. The meetings were often noisy, but productive.

Ramón felt estranged from the process because the new leadership had changed the working climate. The change wasn't negative; it was just different. The climate was now more direct and results-oriented, with the absence of relational and experimental engagement. Ramón felt stifled by the climate change. When I shared my observations with him, he felt liberated. Before he could adapt to the climate, he first had to understand it. Understanding the climate enabled him to function in his uniqueness without building resentment against the process or the other members of the team. Creativity can co-exist with purpose as long as understanding abides and the contributions of both are respected.

Roaming Eyes

Unpredictable spontaneity is often associated with matters of the spirit. It's only reasonable to expect the same when we speak about how God's Spirit is operative in the life of the believer. The spontaneous nature of God's Spirit is evident in scripture. John 3 contains the story of Nicodemus, a Pharisee and member of the Jewish ruling council. Nicodemus recognized Jesus as a teacher of truth, sent by God. Even though Nicodemus was known for his timidity, his recognition of divine power overwhelmed his apprehensions and he sought an interview with the Master under night's cover.

Jesus' response to Nicodemus has been the subject of many interpretations. Commentaries overflow with views about the significance of his reference to water and the Spirit. One of the most intriguing aspects of Jesus' reply is often ignored or addressed only in a cursory manner. Jesus tells Nicodemus: "The wind blows wherever it pleases. You hear its sound, but you cannot tell where it comes from or where it is going. So it is with everyone born of the Spirit" (John 3:8).

He references the erratic wind movement and equates it to a person who is born of the Spirit. Whether Jesus referred to Nicodemus's inability to understand a second birth or the unpredictable nature of Spirit-filled people, the comment attests that people who have experienced a spiritual rebirth in Christ are somewhat difficult to follow or understand. Their pursuits often transcend human logic, just as does the whole notion of a second birth.

The unpredictability sometimes makes it difficult for those who demonstrate high levels of creativity in their demonstration of faith. It's often said they're "marching to the beat of a different drum" when in reality they're acting from a completely different perspective than their more task- and purpose-driven counterparts. Serving with persons who demonstrate such qualities can be extremely rewarding or overwhelmingly frustrating. Their "over-the-edge," "outside-the-box" approach to life and ministry can seem irresponsible and chaotic. Yet, their efforts can yield results that exceed even the most ambitious expectations.

One of the potentially disturbing qualities found in the creative faith-style is the penchant for experimentation and the perception that people who strongly exhibit the creative faith-style are easily distracted. Possessors of creative faith-style love to experiment. They're most comfortable when they know their pursuit of God's will is ungoverned by traditional methods or proven strategies. Failure to engage our experiment-oriented brothers and sisters in new arenas will encourage an already active tendency to leave the present task for the next exciting idea. Think of the ministry team members you know who seem to be easily distracted. They're true believers and committed servants of the Lord, who just seem to have difficulty staying on task. Such believers may even become what I refer to as "ministry hoppers." They volunteer for every committee, project team, and new ministry. Their roaming eyes are a result of unfulfilled appetites for creative faith endeavors.

The tendency to roam can only be tamed by the opportunity to create. Creative believers live by Hebrews 11:6. They truly believe it's impossible to please God without faith, and that faith is demonstrated beyond the boundaries of the commonplace. Creative DNA is resident in all of us, and the creative believer will demonstrate this quality, even if they have to roam to do so.

Don't Box God In

She is unpredictable and sometimes difficult to understand, but she sure does keep things interesting. There's never a dull moment. We'll never forget the time she came to the Church-wide Festival in a Barney suit. Nobody knew who it was, but the children had a fantastic time. Now, every time we have an event, they want to know if Barney is coming. It gives them something to remember. It just goes to show that we need a few people who don't mind taking us beyond the norm. Our picnics aren't just about hamburgers and potato salad anymore. Even Pastor had his picture taken with Barney.

Disorder to Order to Disorder

The creative process means bringing order to disorder. The order that's established represents a new creation. Genesis 1:1-2 states: "In the beginning God created the heavens and the earth. And the earth was without form, and void; and darkness was upon the face of the deep. And the Spirit of God moved upon the face of the waters" (KJV). The earth was without shape and empty while God positioned into a creative posture. The steps that ensued brought order to a shapeless, barren place. From the establishment of light and its separation of darkness to the creation of Eve, every act during the creative process brought order where it didn't exist.

The creative process is replicated in every aspect of life. Productive people engage in creative activity constantly. Many of us are more creative than we realize. Our tendency to associate creativity with artistic activity fails to acknowledge the order that many of us generate on a daily basis in a multitude of situations. We would begin to recognize the creative capacity that resides in us all if we accounted for the times we bring about order on a daily basis. Anyone getting small children off to school every morning is an expert in bringing about order. Getting the young prodigies out of bed, bathed, fed, and to the bus on time is one of the most creative acts parents participate in. God's creative DNA and the ability to bring about order are resident in us all.

Everything created in this world is temporal in nature. Think of the beautiful buildings that are the product of the collaborative, creative efforts of architects and building contractors. Without attention, the order that was established from brick and mortar will in time replicate the condition of the modern-day Roman Coliseum. Order will return to disorder. This reality fuels the actions of believers who have a strong creative faith orientation. Their desire to experiment and bring about newness is never without opportunities. Life, for those who have dominant creative faith-styles, is one big opportunity to bring about newness.

Ministry situations provide numerous opportunities to create new order. Danger exists for ministries that fail to examine existing order and engage in the process of bringing about new order. It's important to unleash the life-giving power of creative activity in every situation. Rather than resisting the tendencies to seek new order, experimentation must be encouraged and embraced as a vital part of ministry efforts. Creative believers must learn to trust what God is doing through their unique ability to seek and bring about new, previously unconsidered realities. There's much in daily life that discourages the pursuit of newness. Submitting to the pressure to avoid what's contrary to the status quo is a sure road to the Roman Coliseum.

Conquering the Dead Zone

Just as everything created in this world is temporary and subject to the natural tendency to deteriorate, creative faith-styles give us a window through which we can peer into the realm of the unseen. It fulfills the true meaning of recreation, which is to refresh and bring about new life. A creative faith-style is one that continuously brings about life. We recognize that there's only one Creator, who enables us to participate through our ability to recreate. The key to sustaining one's ability to recreate is staying in close relationship to the One who initiated creation.

I think back on circumstances when I have experienced creativity lapses. Everyone experiences them, even the most creative. Nothing seems to happen and newness stops flowing. Writers refer to it as "writer's block." The remedies we engage in to cure our brief inability to bring about newness are as diverse as those who experience the problem. The common factor seems to be our inability to remedy the condition on our own. In other words, there's no switch to flip or formula to employ that will guarantee immediate return of the creative flow. So, what's the answer?

The key to sustaining one's ability to recreate is staying in close relationship to the One who initiated creation.

The key to exploiting creative strength is recognizing where it comes from, learning how God's Spirit flows, and working to stay in that flow. Our lapses in creativity aren't because God is napping. We may have lost contact, or we're working with faulty equipment.

It's similar to cell phones; the quality of the phone or finding ourselves in a dead zone causes us to lose our connection. We have to constantly work to improve our "spiritual technology" and eliminate the "dead zones."

I was reminded of this when another minister asked me, "Why are you always writing? You're writing when you're sitting in the pulpit. You're writing when you're in meetings. Every time I see you, you're writing. Why?"

My response was simple: "I'm always writing because God is always talking." My responsibility is to capture as much as I can and use it to create newness whenever possible. The newness may occur by sharing a revelation that blesses or brings comfort to someone else. The newness may come in the form of a unique book idea that adds value to the body of faith-oriented literature. Since God never stops the flow, I have to make sure my equipment is always on and functioning.

Summary

God's spiritual DNA is resident in us all. We're made in divine likeness and endowed with the capacity to reorder the physical world and bring about newness. We have the ability to demonstrate God's character in many ways, the most powerful being our ability to exemplify God's love. Demonstrating God's love can bring about newness in situations that have otherwise been declared hopeless. Relationships are made new through sacrificial love. Potential is realized when we're encouraged by such love, which unleashes creativity of all kinds because it removes the barrier of self-condemnation.

Creativity and learning are closely related, both enabling us to transcend recognized boundaries. Creativity takes us beyond the norm into a realm that has never been considered. Learning is a similar exercise because it transcends what's currently known. Both endeavors can be unsettling. That's why those who possess strong creative faith-styles seem to be able to "go out on limbs" from which others shy away. Miracles lay in wait in the realm of the yet discovered.

Creative faith thrives in certain environments. The unstructured nature of creativity is most active when boundaries are limitless. If a person needs structure in order to feel productive, chances are they don't express creativity in their demonstrations of faith. Structure and routine create dead zones for those who demonstrate creative faith-styles. It doesn't mean that those who are minimally creative in their faith never bring about anything new. It simply means that when the climate is right, creative faith flourishes.

The tendency to flourish when boundaries are minimal causes those who are highly creative in their faith to seem unfocused. They may move from idea to idea, activity to activity, in a manner that seems to be completely illogical. This is simply the nature of the creative in their application of faith. Creativity drives their quest for newness. Faith drives their ability to move in unproven areas seemingly without concern. One might imagine how this influences the interactions between those who possess creative faith-styles and those who are more action- or responsibility-oriented. The interaction has the potential for frustration and confusion unless understanding of styles is achieved.

Order is often achieved through the creative process. Newness involves taking elements of creation that are seemingly unrelated and fashioning them into something new that expresses value. It's our constant quest to subdue the earth (Gen. 1:28) and make it alive through a continual process of recreation. This process requires faith and trust, the ability to believe that something can always emerge from nothing. When creative tendencies are combined with faith in an omnipotent God, new meaning is given to Paul's declaration about Christ, "I can do all things through him who strengthens me" (Phil. 4:13 NRSV).

Discussion Guide

1. List characteristics that are indicators of God's spiritual DNA in you life.

2. Describe situations in which God's love has brought newness to situations that seemed hopeless. Identify opportunities to apply God's love in a creative manner.

3. Describe a situation in which you were able to be most creative in exercising your faith. What was the situation? What made it more conducive to a creative faith-style? How might you work in current situations to make them more conducive to a creative style of faith?

4. Identify "dead zones" in your ability to hear God's voice. What are some ways that you will attempt to conquer the dead zones?

5. Has there ever been a time when you moved from idea to idea, or project to project in short time periods? Where you operating in a creative faith-style, or being irresponsible?

CHAPTER 7

Being All That You Can Be

I often reflect about the great value in my rural upbringing, the experiences and relationships that are endemic to the "country boy" lifestyle. One such experience is the planting season. My family managed to plant a huge garden every year, even though my parents weren't from farming families. Hard, physical labor was the order of the day. The labor was especially rigorous because the mountainous terrain made the use of tractors or other automated equipment impossible. The five large plots of land were prepared by hand every spring. March and April were the months of blisters, calluses, healthy appetites, and restful sleep.

The exposure to the agrarian lifestyle gave me a good understanding of the horticultural process. I knew planting, harvesting, and everything in between, but my youthful perspective didn't always afford me a healthy appreciation for the experience. I had no concept of the life-lessons that would prepare me for so many other endeavors. However, preparing soil, planting seed, extracting weeds, protecting against insects and other crop-eating creatures, and harvesting, all taught me agricultural skills and valuable lessons about life, relationships, and closeness with God.

Take a few moments to survey your life for indications of growth. Are you the same person you were 10 years ago? You have changed physically, emotionally, and spiritually. Many changes are positive indicators of growth. Because growth is usually viewed as positive, people seek to advance, empower, and otherwise enhance their abilities based on their perceived growth. It's believed that those who are able to assess and manipulate their growth in positive ways will be more effective in all of their endeavors, including efforts to serve the Lord. As a result, the way in which believers approach the topic of growth and advancement is critical to how we live out our faith and service.

Barbara is an excellent example of an achievement-oriented believer. She's a committed member of a local congregation. Everyone admires Barbara because of her knowledge of God's Word and the way she willingly shares her understanding of scripture. Nothing pleases her more than when she's able to direct someone to a passage that addresses their concern or brings them comfort. Barbara also has a voracious appetite for educational endeavors that she believes will enhance her already keen knowledge of the Word. She demonstrated her motivation to learn from the time she joined St. Mark's Church. She proudly completed the new member's classes, immediately joined a Bible study, found time to participate in a discipleship group, and regularly attends conferences sponsored by other ministry organizations. Barbara's approach to her faith and service are intentional and ambitious. She spends time feeding and nurturing her understanding of God, believing that her understanding will enable her to serve God more effectively and strengthen her relationship with the Lord. There's no one I know who brings 2 Timothy 2:15 to life in the unique way Barbara does.

If the description of Barbara fits you, your dominant faith-style is probably growth/achievement-oriented. The concern for growth is usually perceived as a good trait, yet as with anything, there are always cautions. My agricultural experience taught me that too much nourishment can

Growth that produces good spiritual fruit must be intentional, managed, and sustained with an understanding that the goal is to become all that God desires us to be and to fulfill God's purpose.

damage the soil and kill the crops. Growth that produces good spiritual fruit must be intentional, managed, and sustained with an understanding that the goal is to become all that God desires us to be and to fulfill God's purpose. Let's examine the intricacies of what it means to grow in faith and service to the Lord.

Inhibitors

There are many potential inhibitors to a person's growth. The causes can be obvious and immediately noticeable, or very obscure, complex, and difficult to detect. The first step to diagnosing inhibitors is realizing that they can be internal as well as external. Environmental conditions, as well as mental and spiritual conditions, can equally contribute to one's inability to grow. Achievement-oriented believers find ways to minimize the negative impact of growth inhibitors.

Environmental conditions are restricted to the people with whom we interact and the things around us. We have to be careful because of the subtlety of certain environmental growth inhibitors. Growth can be thwarted by the very efforts that are employed to foster it. Efforts to mentor can actually become a hindrance to growth if the mentoring provides artificial security that never encourages the assisted to develop qualities that will increase their capabilities. This can be as damaging as being in a place where growth doesn't occur. That anything at rest tends to remain at rest makes it possible to become very comfortable in surroundings not promoting growth.

I once worked for an organization that had a reputation as a great place to be employed. They offered great benefits, a recession-resistant industry, and many other reasonably good perks. Most employees had worked there for many years. The only disturbing observation was that many of the long-term employees worked in the same positions when they retired that they worked in when they started. The organization had many great qualities, but it wasn't known for promoting growth. It was easy for people to become comfortable and satisfied in their positions, never seeking to advance—a situation that an achievement-oriented believer would never tolerate.

There are times when the deterrents to growth aren't in our surroundings; they reside within. The internal inhibitors to growth are often learned behaviors. We're born with a natural proclivity for exploring, learning, and internalizing new experiences. Developing habits that are contrary to these tendencies will inhibit one's ability to achieve. Think of the way we attempt to encourage children to become high achievers. We read the latest research on child development, purchase educational toys, and try to help children develop good study habits and minimize idle time. We attempt to enhance their natural ability to learn, achieve, and overcome the inhibitors to achievement that are encountered throughout life.

Regardless of whether the source of growth inhibitors is internal or external, they have the capacity to keep us from being all that we can be in Christ. An intentional effort is required to minimize their influence. Achievement-oriented faith is based on the belief that growth and achievement glorify the God who is the object of our faith. Faith and focused effort will help to break the bonds of growth inhibitors.

We're on the Grow

There are three services every Sunday. Every service is filled to capacity. Before the end of the day, 7,000 worshipers have sat in the sanctuary. A service in which no new converts commit their lives to Christ is a rarity. Increases in membership are between 50 to 100 members each month. Do you want to go beyond the numbers? There are Bible studies for every level, every day of the week. There is a small-group Discipleship program with over 800 people enrolled to take on the three-year commitment. There are also conferences throughout the year that focus on the specific issues faced by men, women, youth, and more specific subgroups.

Behind it all, you'll find a growth faith-style and achievement-oriented leadership. A growing ministry is often led by people who have a propensity for growth.

Preparing the Soil

Sometimes we wonder why one person grows and another remains stagnant when they're exposed to the same opportunities, have access to the same resources, and listen to the same preaching. Yet, one person grows in Christ, and the other seems to wither on the vine. Just as there are many inhibitors to spiritual growth, there are also contributors. No single factor guarantees advancement towards mature faith. As fervently as we may try to find a formula for growth that works for every person, in every situation, the formula just simply doesn't exist. It requires hard work and diligence to bring about the potential for growth.

Those who are achievement-oriented seem to have a keen understanding of the work required for growth. They have a single-minded purpose to complete the day a little further along than when they began. Many achievement-oriented believers spend inordinate amounts of time preparing to move to the next level of achievement. After a while, their preparation begins to blend with what's considered their achievements. It begins to appear as if their lives are one fluid achievement after another. However, they have been so focused on advancing that every activity becomes preparation for the next. All of this is done with an unshakeable belief that their achievements glorify and are pleasing in the sight of God.

Spiritual growth is much like preparing to grow crops. Nothing will survive in rocky soil. Jesus made reference to this truth concerning seed planting in the parable of the sower: "Some fell on stony places, where they had not much earth: and forthwith they sprung up because they had no deepness of earth. And when the sun was up, they were scorched; and because they had no root, they withered away" (Matt. 13:5, 6 KJV). The implication is that the land must be cleared for growth to be sustained. The "soil" of our hearts and minds must be cleared on a regular basis for real advancements to occur. Think of the obstacles that seem to inhibit our ability to walk closely with God and excel in faith and service. Some people are plagued by memories of past experiences; others spend time in environments that aren't conducive to growth. Regardless of the reason, the proper conditions must exist for growth to occur.

How do we prepare ourselves for spiritual growth and Christian service? There are many ways to prepare the spiritual landscape. I have come to really appreciate the benefits of preparation, thanks to the guidance and teaching of my pastor, Rev. Dr. Walter S. Thomas, of the New Psalmist Baptist Church in Baltimore. To the surprise of some church staff members, Pastor Thomas mandated that everyone construct an altar in her or his office. He added that it didn't have to be elaborate, just representative of what we desire to present to the Lord. You can imagine the diversity in our efforts. The final products were as different as the personalities of the staff members. We were further instructed to spend time at our altars in prayer at the beginning of each day. This time was to be in addition to any other devotional activity occurring before reaching the church. He even went as far as to suggest that we place "do not disturb" signs on our doors during devotional time. We were all encouraged by the fact that he visited each office and prayed with each staff member at his or her altar. Even though it wasn't clear to me at the time, I now know that Pastor Thomas was preparing us for growth. He was preparing the landscape of the ministry by engaging its servants in personal preparation. I'll be eternally grateful for the lesson I learned from the experience. The fruit of the ministry and our individual lives will forever be sweeter because we learned how to prepare for growth and achievement.

Getting Off to a Good Start

The ability to sustain growth is predicated on getting off to a good start. Growth will not last unless saplings are nurtured and given the opportunity to develop strong roots. People who demonstrate achievement-oriented faith often display nurturing qualities in their pursuit of goals. They cautiously take their first steps toward achievement, realizing that setbacks are more difficult to overcome in the early stages of any endeavor. We protect our children for that very reason. We know that much of their maturity and growth potential depends upon our ability to provide support in their formative years. This truth demonstrates itself over and over again in the lives of those who realize consistent growth in Christ.

Three principles predicate great beginnings: covering, nourishment, and space. Growth is minimized in the absence of any one of these principles. Every effort to grow in new areas or launch new faith endeavors must be guided by them. Covering refers to protection. We must vigilantly protect what hasn't matured. It's not just a matter of isolating our concerns or ourselves during formative stages, because too much protection can be as harmful as too little. However, it suggests that special attention be given at the appropriate time. Young children, for example, will never gain the confidence necessary to grow if the parents never give opportunities to test their abilities. I remember many occasions when we observed our children from an undetectable position to give them a sense of achievement. Even though we were poised to intervene if they were overwhelmed, giving them a chance to operate on their own encouraged growth. Although cover can hinder when inappropriately applied, it can protect when appropriate.

The second principle of great beginnings is good nourishment. Newness requires nourishment. From newborn babies to newborn believers, they all require good nourishment. The absence of essential nutrients makes us vulnerable to infection and disease. This is very much a necessity for growth because by definition growth creates a strain on the system. Growth implies movement beyond the norm. Growth will bring on more responsibilities, activity, and effort. A failure to receive proper nourishment during such a time jeopardizes the potential achievements. Think of the science experiments we used to do in elementary school. I remember more than one occasion that required the planting of seeds in paper cups. A few seeds, a couple of paper cups, and a couple of scoops of dirt made for a fantastic laboratory. If you were ever fortunate enough to engage in this great process of scientific inquiry, you remember that the hypothesis was based on the understanding that plants deprived of nutrition, water, and light would be less healthy than those who received an ample supply. Well, the hypothesis most often proved true, except for a few budding scientists whose seeds never germinated for other reasons. Little did we realize that we were learning truths that would have much wider implications. Spiritual, physical, and emotional nourishment is absolutely critical, especially during the early stages of growth.

Our horticultural analogy provides a helpful image for demonstrating the space principle. My wife was repotting a flower one day when our daughter interrupted her with a question, "Mommy, why didn't you just put the flower in that pot the first time? Then you wouldn't have to do that now." My wife explained: "The plant needs the correct amount of space for the roots to grow properly. It wouldn't have been good to place it in a pot that was too large when first planted. It has now grown roots that need room to spread. The flower will never bloom and become as beautiful as it could be if the roots don't have room to spread and get the maximum amount of nourishment possible." Our daughter seemed quite satisfied with the answer and proceeded to ask, "Mommy, will I need more room so I can grow?" My wife answered, "You certainly will, sweetheart. And we'll try to make sure that you have it."

Growing Seasons

We're all subject to cycles and seasons. The sun doesn't shine 24 hours a day. Those of us who live far enough from the equator experience hot, warm, cool, and cold seasons. Even those who live in the more tropical regions of the earth usually experience seasons of rain and dryness. Growth and achievement are also subject to similar cyclical patterns. I can easily identify periods in my life when I seemed to be caught in a growth phase that was beyond my understanding and control. Likewise, I can remember periods when I felt stagnant and unproductive. To attempt to control the cycles of growth would be much like attempting weather control. You can't always tell when the seasons are changing. It's just best to be prepared when it does.

Achievement-oriented believers seem to understand the cycles. Like skilled planters, they understand seasonal timing. Those who don't understand the principle of seasons often frustrate themselves by attempting to accomplish something for a season that hasn't arrived. This often happens for those who yearn for instant success. They push and push, and find themselves out of sync with the movement of God's will and purpose. Their ideas about success and what "should" happen cloud their ability to listen and interpret the season. There's a way to practice "spiritual meteorology" and have a sense of what the forecast says about the climate. This isn't predicting the moves of God; however, it's a matter of listening to what God is saying, watching the way God is moving, and being ready to participate in the prevailing season.

I've observed the seasonal movement of God in my preaching. During my early stages, I was long on desire and short on ability. I prayed constantly that my preaching would become more effective so that people would come to greater understanding and relationship with the Lord through the preached word. God's reply was that my preaching ability was subject to seasonal evolution and divine guidance. God was making changes in me that would have a profound impact on my messages.

I also received advice during this time from those who were "more seasoned" in ministry. The advice ran the gamut from preparation, to the use of specific commentaries, to the suggestion that improvement was a function of regularity in the pulpit. I heard it all. However, God was using the experience to teach me a lesson about preordained seasons. To accomplish this God gave me periods of silence, times when I wasn't preaching. Sometimes the divinely imposed silence lasted for months. Even invitations that were normally extended during these times didn't come. While such an experience would normally have been disturbing, I had a strange peace about it all, as if God were saying to me, "I need you to be quiet right now because I'm doing something special."

When you're synchronized with the seasons of God, you will be blessed beyond your wildest expectations and those around you will be the beneficiaries of what God has done.

At the end of each period, God brought about changes and growth in my preaching that I can't explain and for which I can't take credit. It's growth that has proven to be seasonal and divinely orchestrated.

I thank God for lessons about seasonal growth and maturity. You can't rush it. There isn't anything you can do to override it, and my experience suggests that there's nothing that can exceed it.

When you're synchronized with the seasons of God, you will be blessed beyond your wildest expectations and those around you will be the beneficiaries of what God has done. Don't miss your season!

When Do I Rest?

Rest is important to growth and achievement. We often get so involved in the activities associated with achievement that rest becomes a secondary concern. However, we have to remind ourselves that lack of rest diminishes our mental focus, impairs our judgment, impedes our memory, erodes our patience, and contributes to our physical decline. In other words, failing to rest is counterproductive to our efforts to grow and achieve. This doesn't imply that we shouldn't strive or extend ourselves. Yet, it means that care must be taken so we get the maximum benefit out of each effort we make to grow.

A good friend of mine urgently approached me with a great problem. He was concerned about his devotional time with God. He was troubled because he seemed to fall asleep whenever he took time to pray or just spend time talking to God. He lamented further by saying, "At the least, God must consider me to be terribly rude." As we talked about this concern, the Lord led me to ask some probing questions. I asked about his work schedule, what time he awakened in the morning, and when he went to bed at night. It was no surprise to find out that he was averaging about four or five hours of sleep each night. He even sought partially to justify rising an hour earlier to spend time with God. I assured him that God would much rather talk to him when he was rested and mentally lucid. Then I encouraged him to get some rest. We cheat ourselves and fail to give God our best when we don't take time to give our bodies and minds rest. The human body and mind are limited in capacity and must be replenished. Rest is an essential part of a holistically healthy lifestyle that should include exercise, good nutrition, and knowledgeable medical care.

There are several suggestions about finding time for rest. The first step toward better rest is eliminating as many stressors in your life as possible. Stress is a major contributor to our inability to rest. If you're one of the people who have difficulty turning your mind off at night, chances are your life is too stressful. How can you rest when your mind is racing from thought to thought? It's unrealistic to suggest that you will be able to eliminate all stress from your life, but if you can't eliminate the stressor, change your thinking regarding the stressor. You have the ability to change your perspective. You'll be surprised how much stress can be eliminated that way.

Second, we must set priorities and stick to them. One reason we're so fatigued at the end of the day is because we're like the proverbial "chicken without a head," running around aimlessly from situation to situation, never accomplishing what's most important. You'll be surprised how much better you rest when you've set a few worthy priorities and accomplished them all.

Third, eliminate your distractions. I used to have the terrible habit of trying to do too many things at once. This is the age of multitasking, but there's something to be said for doing one thing at a time and doing it well. Work on the one thing. Everything else is a distraction at that moment. It's also very tiring to correct all of the mistakes made when we aren't focused. Lastly, just say, "Yes." Busy people have a habit of automatically saying, "I can't" when someone suggests they take a break. I have seldom regretted when I have submitted to such a suggestion. Those times represent some of the most fun I've ever had.

Achievement-oriented faith is driven by the belief that God is pleased when we grow. I believe whole-heartedly that God is pleased when we grow and mature in faith. However, we have to make sure that we're growing in a healthy manner so that God gets our best, not what we struggle to give with a fatigued mind and body. Let's be all that we can be and give God all that we can give by making sure our stamina is fully intact.

Growth Hormones

The purpose of a hormone is to stimulate or excite. Personal growth and achievement must be stimulated and encouraged. Growth will eventually diminish and come to an end without stimulation of some kind. I have observed this phenomenon in my attempt to stay physically fit. My goal is to maintain a balance between my cardiovascular exercise and strength training. In my best efforts, I'm able to run five miles, five days of each week, and lift weights three or four days of each week. It's easier for me to maintain my running routine because I have a treadmill in my home. However, the weight training is more of a challenge because it requires going to a training facility. It's easy for one or two days of missed workouts to turn into one or two weeks. There's an obvious decline in my strength and stamina following a period without lifting. The lack of stimulation sets the stage for a decline and a necessity to rebuild strength.

Any attempt to grow requires constant activity to sustain advancements. Achievement-oriented believers are in a constant state of activity with achievement of some kind as the ultimate aim. The achievement goal is expanded once it becomes an accomplishment. Much like creative faith, achievement faith continuously places the believer in a situation of transcendence. There's always a need to go beyond current capabilities. The growth cycle is extended by the expansion of goals. For example, one week I was able to comfortably achieve 15 repetitions with 90-pound weights. In order to increase my capacity, it was necessary to increase the weights or increase the repetitions. In either case, I had to move toward levels of activity beyond my current accomplishments.

Another weight-training principle is very useful for understanding truths about growth. Muscle growth is maximized when "muscle confusion" techniques are used. Muscle confusion occurs when the routine is changed regularly. The technique doesn't allow the muscles to get used to the same exercises. The same technique must be applied when attempting to achieve growth in other areas of our lives. Faith grows when we engage in activities we aren't familiar with. It also grows when we approach familiar activities in a different manner. When we find ourselves beyond recognized capabilities, or outside our comfort zones, faith is exercised.

Faith in Christ is a catalyst for personal growth, taking us beyond the routine into new experiences and untapped potential. Faith is the spiritual growth hormone that stimulates deeper experiences in Christ. We're able to witness what we may never have seen and accomplish what has been beyond our grasp. Jesus makes it clear that the ability to transcend known capabilities rests in him: "If you can?" said Jesus, "Everything is possible for him who believes" (Mark 9:23). All things are possible if you stay focused and place your faith in the One who is able to make a difference. Life will become more exciting, with dreams and aspirations materializing. You will begin to feel the strength that emerges from stepping beyond personal trials and tribulations, giving God glory and praise every step of the way.

Summary

Achievement-oriented faith takes the believer into continuous growth and new experiences in Christ. In spite of all of the deterrents to growth, faith in Christ and the knowledge that our achievements glorify him help to push past the boundaries of existing capabilities.

Personal growth is very analogous to horticultural growth. As with any attempt to grow healthy crops, there must be a period of preparation if maximum growth is going to occur. Getting off to a good start is absolutely critical. We're most vulnerable in the early stages of growth. Care must be taken to nurture growth attempts until the effort becomes stable and strong enough to survive inevitable difficulties.

We must also work to recognize periods in our lives when conditions are more conducive to growth. Some circumstances are within our control, but there are many situations we have no power to influence. Learning to recognize and use growing seasons to our advantage is critical for maximizing growth. Farmers don't sow seeds in the winter because the timing doesn't make sense, and the desired results are unlikely.

Christian maturity is a goal that we never fully fulfill. There's always room for growth, to transcend and go beyond current abilities. Faith is the catalyst for growth, and growth is the key to becoming all you can be in Christ.

Discussion Guide

1. Describe the areas in which you've experienced your most dramatic growth during the past five years.

2. Discuss the factors that contributed to your growth in these areas. Discuss the factors that inhibited your growth.

3. In what growth initiatives are you currently involved that are in their early stages? Discuss the steps you'll take to nurture these initiatives through their formative stages.

4. Describe your most productive growth season. What were some of the circumstances that made the season productive?

5. Discuss your strategy for rest and relaxation. Describe your performance when rested. Describe your performance when fatigued.

PART THREE

Putting Faith-Styles to Work

CHAPTER 8

The Servant Response
Faith-Style Model

The Servant Resource Faith-Style Model (SRFS Model) is a visual representation of the relationship between faith and service as well as a framework for the analysis of faith-styles, enabling people to realize how their beliefs influence the way they render service (see Figure 2). Leaders may also find the framework useful as a leadership development tool and a framework for analyzing relationship issues on ministry teams.

Figure 2
The Servant Resource Faith-Style Model

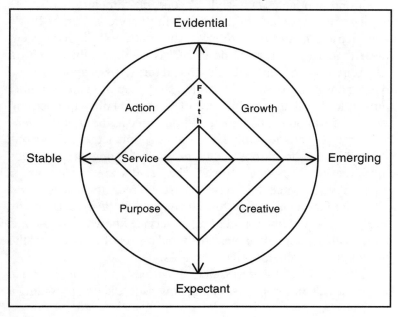

Before examining the model in detail, I'll set the stage by providing a brief overview. The model consists of a vertical axis representing faith and a horizontal axis representing service. They represent the spiritual nature of faith and the earthly function of service. The extreme of each axis also bears significance. The upper extreme of the faith axis is *evidential*, demonstrated by objective activity that one believes will lead to progress. The lower extreme of the faith axis is expectant, which is observed in spontaneous expressions of hope that facilitate progress toward a desired objective. The two extremes of the service axis are also identified by the unique way in which service is executed. When facing the model, the extreme left of the service axis is identified as *stable*. The extreme right of the service axis is identified as *emerging*.

The two axes represent the manner in which faith and service are rendered. The four quadrants formed by the two intersecting axes represent four different faith-styles. The description of each faith-style is the result of a unique synthesis of the extremes of each axis. First, the combination of evidential faith and stable service form a faith-style quadrant that's identified as the *action faith-style*. Stable service and evidential faith constitute an action or responsibility-oriented faith-style. Second, the combination of stable service and expectant faith form a faith-style quadrant that's identified as the *purpose faith-style*. This time the steady, consistent linear rendering of service described as stable combines with a different type of faith that's characterized by spontaneous expressions of hope. They constitute a purpose or vision-oriented faith-style. Third, the combination of expectant faith and emerging service form another quadrant that's identified as the *creative faith-style*. In this scenario, faith exercised as spontaneous expressions of hope leading to purpose combines with the unexpected needs and situational service efforts. The results are a creative or experiment-oriented faith-style. Lastly, emerging service and evidential faith converge to form the *growth faith-style*. Here, the steady, consistent linear rendering of service known as stable has united with the unpredictable, situational aspect of faith to form the growth or achievement-oriented faith-style.

The results of the various combinations of faith and service provide a system for understanding how people serve, providing a valuable framework for advancing the cause of ministry for the future. The more aware we become of ourselves, the easier it is to submit to God's calling and direction. Submission helps us to be more productive.

The Heavenly Nature of Faith

The extremes of the evidential and expectancy axis represent different facets of faith. Faith is the linkage between our existence in a physical realm of tangible reality and the ethereal realm of the unknown. Faith provides impetus for action and is the evidence of one's beliefs. It's also a foundation for hope, an intense feeling that desired events will come to pass. Those who exercise faith are blessed (John 20:29), meaning they're endowed with divine favor and spiritual benefit. God confers goodness on the recipient of divine blessing.

I'm intrigued by the relationship of the disciple Thomas with Jesus. He's best known for his inability to believe that Jesus had risen from the dead. His slowness to believe earned him the nickname "Doubting Thomas." Yet, he also demonstrated great compassion and love for the Master. It was Thomas who encouraged everyone to prepare to die with Jesus when they were informed of his intention to go to Judea, a place where Jesus had been threatened with stoning (John 11:16). Thomas was also the one who questioned Jesus about where he was going when Jesus explained his departure and plans to prepare a place for his followers (John 14:5). Despite Thomas's reluctance to believe, we can be grateful for the clarity of Jesus' response. We're blessed because we believe without seeing. We're the recipients of divine favor and spiritual benefit.

The gift of faith and the spiritual benefit that it provides can be summarized by one word: *life*. In John 6:63, Jesus states: "The Spirit gives life; the flesh counts for nothing. The words I have spoken to you are spirit and they are life." The evidential and expectancy dimensions of faith contribute to the manifestation of life. Our service is more animated, our relationships more vibrant, and we're better able to resist the situations that cause us to become ineffective. Faith is the gift from above that links us to spiritual benefit.

The Earthly Nature of Service

People of faith have a responsibility that is supported in scripture to serve and improve every situation encountered. This isn't an easy assignment, for we live in a world corrupted by sin. We regularly face situations that challenge our emotions and defy our ability to make sense of them. Yet, we're charged with the responsibility to be a light in dark places. Service rendered to humankind by a follower of Christ is service rendered unto the Lord. The act of service is simply a physical manifestation of a person's relationship with God and commitment to the charge of serving. It's the relationship born of faith that inspires acts of service.

When speaking of the final judgment, Jesus indicates that a time will come when all will have to account for acts of service. He said:

> "For I was hungry and you gave me something to eat, I was thirsty and you gave me something to drink, I was a stranger and you invited me in, I needed clothes and you clothed me, I was sick and you looked after me, I was in prison and you came to visit me."
>
> Then the righteous will answer him, "Lord, when did we see you hungry and feed you, or thirsty and give you something to drink? When did we see you a stranger and invite you in, or needing clothes and clothe you? When did we see you sick or in prison and go to visit you?"
>
> Then the King will reply, "I tell you the truth, whatever you did for one of the least of these brothers of mine, you did for me." (Matt. 25:35-40)

The serving mandate is solidified by the fact that Jesus imposed himself in the place of the least. He indicated that service, even to those who would be considered the least by human standards, is valuable.

We take ourselves out of the flow of God's plan if we make no effort to affect the world around us, by serving as the "salt of the earth" (Matt. 5:13). We're to preserve, purify, and serve as an improvement agent. Ministry is a con-

Ministry is a continuous intervent...
into the affairs of a world
that needs hope and life.
Service is the tool
that every ministry agent can use
to fulfill the mandate
to bring light to dark places.

tinuous intervention into the affairs of a world that needs hope and life. Service is the tool that every ministry agent can use to fulfill the mandate to bring light to dark places.

Evidential Versus Expectant Faith

The evidential nature of faith is demonstrated by objective activity that one believes will lead to progress. Acts of faith are encouraged by past experiences. Faith is strengthened as a person increasingly engages in acts of faith. The relationship between the personal servant and the One in whom that person's faith resides is also strengthened. Faith is continually necessary because of new situations and new challenges. Even though past experiences provide evidence of the efficacy of faith, every day is filled with situations that are new or slightly different.

Examples of our efforts to serve can be drawn from routine circumstances. Many of my days in the ministry go from 9 A.M. until 9 P.M., with no two being the same. I handle numerous voice-mail messages, e-mail messages, and meetings, but again, the ever-evolving nature of ministry means that no two are the same. People frequently contact me with prayer concerns, yet every situation requires a unique approach. The evidential faith perspective lets me know that God's grace is sufficient and that God's power is indeed made perfect in my weakness (2 Cor. 12:9). I've seen God provide so many times that I'm compelled to step beyond the threshold of my limitations with an increasing measure of boldness. This is the evidence of what I can't see.

Acts of evidential faith are more linear and logical than acts born of expectancy. This doesn't mean that linear and logical acts of faith require a lesser degree of trust. Faith is still, and always will be, a subjective act by virtue of its focus on the unseen, but the activities that result from belief are based on a thought process. In other words, we decide to believe based on a process of reasoning that prompts us to engage in a subjective practice that governs our lives. Does this mean that we're haphazard and reckless in the way we live? No, our actions are soundly based in trust, proven throughout the ages. Faith has a track record of moving people beyond their fears, empowering them to strive for better, and holding them together during difficult times. We never know if what we're going to face is new, unexpected, or even unpleasant. But through it all, we have evidence, beyond a shadow of a doubt, that faith will help us.

The expectant nature of faith is observed in spontaneous expressions of hope that facilitate progress toward a desired objective. In the same manner that faith from the evidential perspective is based on a linear thought process and encouraged by evidence, the expectancy faith perspective is much more spontaneous. It's a move into the unknown born of hope, when there's no evidence or history. In some ways, this could be considered a deeper level of faith. I'm reluctant to identify it as deeper because I believe that both faith perspectives are essential. It's like saying that quantitative information is more valuable than qualitative. The people who make that claim don't understand they play different roles in the common purpose of advancing knowledge. Evidential and expectancy perspectives are different manifestations of the same requirement.

There will be times when the expectancy expression of faith is absolutely essential. Abraham is perhaps the best example of expectancy faith perspectives: "Against all hope, Abraham in hope believed and so became the father of many nations" (Rom. 4:18a). There's no evidence from the past that remotely suggests Abraham would be called "father" by anyone. In fact, the account adds: "Without weakening in his faith, he faced the fact that his body was as good as dead—since he was about a hundred years old— and that Sarah's womb was also dead" (Rom. 4:19). He fully recognized that he and Sarah hadn't been able to conceive. His body and her womb are described as dead. Still, Abraham was able to make a decision to trust God for delivering on the promise.

Evidential and expectancy perspectives work hand-in-hand. That we all tend to operate more comfortably from one perspective has no bearing on the fact that the actions still constitute acts of faith. We're always better rounded when we operate comfortably from either perspective. This enables us to exercise faith with efficacy and in a manner that's relevant to the situation. People who possess a strong faith gift are usually good at switching between perspectives, never appearing to be paralyzed by the lack of faith. They're able to "play the cards they're dealt," utilizing faith to make the best of their "hand." God is pleased in the process and servant potential is unleashed in a powerful way.

Stable Versus Emerging Service

The stable dimension of service is a more structured approach requiring intense planning and incremental implementation. Those who operate on this end of the service spectrum are planners from start to finish. The stable aspect of service conveys order, process, standardization, and authority. Servants who serve in this mode are valuable when control is perceived as necessary.

An important aspect of the service continuum is its relevance to the environment. The same is true for the faith continuum. However, the service axis represents the earthly dimension of the model. Therefore, environment is even more important. Stable approaches to service are more compatible with stable environments. The less the environment changes, the more appropriate stable approaches to service will be.

Stable service is also characterized by prescriptive offerings, one in which the person offering the service presumes to know what type of service is best for the recipient. For example, a ministry volunteer offers to visit a nursing home. Prior to their departure, the volunteer writes an itinerary of activities that they will execute with the people they visit. The ministry volunteer assumes to know what's best for the people they will encounter, and no consideration has been given to contingencies. If a need arises to deviate from the pre-determined plan, frustration sets in, and the servant may ultimately withdraw from the mission without accomplishing the objectives. Nothing is inherently wrong with the prescriptive approach. In fact, it's probably a good idea to have a pre-determined itinerary. However, problems may arise if there's an unwillingness to modify the plan based on situational encounters. Contingency plans keep the servant from becoming too rigid.

Stable approaches to service are also characterized by rigid chains of command. Those on the stable end of the spectrum are more likely to create authoritarian hierarchies among fellow servants. Leaders in the service hierarchy have authority over the activities of volunteers. Failure to comply with service standards, policies, and procedures will result in retribution and possibly dismissal from the service environment. This approach doesn't encourage deviations from the norm. Also, communication is limited between different service groups or teams because everything is subject to authorization.

Emerging service results from unpredictable needs that require situational approaches. This approach to service is more fluid than the stable approach. Service isn't prescriptive in nature, but is approached from a client-led perspective. Service is seen as the response to a unique need that's articulated by the person being served. From this perspective, service needs remain unpredictable. The servant approaches the service opportunity with no preconceived notion about what will be discovered or what interventions will be necessary. The servant must maintain a cadre of interventions that are totally dictated by need.

Service at this end of the continuum stays compatible with rapidly changing environments. Servants respond rapidly and adjust to various, unexpected situations. I again emphasize that one perspective isn't better than the other. They're two parts of a whole, and both parts are equally relevant as they're measured against the environment. Ministry staffs function more efficiently when they're able to respond from the appropriate perspective. Different servants on the team have strengths in different areas, which all work to the advancement of effective ministry.

Elements of
Servant Resource Faith-Styles

Servant resource faith-style elements are displayed in detail in appendix C. The elements are described in terms of faith orientation, assumptions, common experiences, personality traits, strengths, and limitations. There are four faith orientations that correspond to the four faith-styles. Servants with dominant action faith-styles are said to be responsibility-oriented. Servants with dominant purpose faith-styles are described as vision-oriented. Those with a dominant creative faith-style are described as experiment-oriented. Servants with a dominant growth faith-style are said to be achievement-oriented. Faith orientation is meant to further describe each faith-style.

The word assumption describes the servant's understanding and application of faith. Each faith-style is based on a specific perspective or understanding regarding the utility of faith. Demonstrations of faith occur when assumptions about who God is and what God can do, and about the gift of faith becoming so compelling that we take action. An assumption is no more than a belief that's accepted without the benefit of objective information. The definition of assumption sounds a great deal like faith, because faith requires assumptions.

There are also common experiences that arise from particular faith-styles. Those who possess particular styles as dominant have common experiences that are the result of their common style. For example, those who demonstrate a dominant action faith-style feel like the "activity police," often having to bring people back to the task at hand. They see action as consistent with faithfulness. Therefore, they find themselves attempting to get people back on track. Every style is subject to common experiences.

Certain personality traits are common in people with particular styles. Personality is the behavioral patterns that identify a person, which are reflective of their mental and emotional make up. Personality traits are a good indicator of faith-styles. While it's not impossible for faith-style and personality inconsistencies to occur, it's not likely. It should also be noted that a person with a particular faith-style might possess some of the personality traits that are identified as consistent with their style. The number of personality traits that are actually consistent will depend on the strength of their dominant style.

Strengths are the positive qualities that help the personal servant, as well as any ministry team on which they might serve, effectively accomplish goals. Limitations are those characteristics viewed as less desirable. Identifying strengths and limitations give people a framework for examining behaviors they may want to accentuate or change. It enables them to be more effective in their attempts to grow and understand others with whom they serve.

Summary

The Servant Resource Faith-Style Model provides a framework that enables individual servants and ministry team members to serve more effectively. It brings the elements of faith and service together in a way that helps them navigate the sometimes difficult waters of Christian service, earthly relationships, and their relationship with God. The four-quadrant design of the model isn't unique; however, it adequately captures the elements of faith and service and places them in an easily understood perspective.

Faith is the key element in our relationship with God. Faith is empty in the absence of God's omnipotence, and the gift of faith carries spiritual benefit. The SRFS Model identifies faith as evidential or expectant in nature, evidence of what we don't see and the substance of our hope. The earthly nature of service gives reference to our obligation to serve society and make the world a better place. This is the impetus that undergirds our service efforts, endeavors that are born out of our faith. Each faith-style is depicted as a unique combination of faith and service perspectives.

The elements of faith-styles can be understood more clearly in the context of faith orientations, assumptions, common experiences, personality traits, strengths, and limitations. They give servants detailed information required to understand particular tendencies of each style. Service becomes more effective when we understand the underlying principles of the unique way faith is exercised.

Discussion Guide

1. Which faith perspective best describes your way of exercising faith?

2. Which service perspective best describes your way of rendering service?

3. Describe the ministry environment in which you serve. Is it more conducive to the stable or emerging approach to service?

4. Think of your moments of doubt and describe how each faith-style would address your doubt.

5. Which faith-style best describes you?

CHAPTER 9

Understanding Faith-Inspired Responsibility

His nickname is "Mr. Dependable"—always on time, always follows through on a commitment, and always calls to keep others informed. He's known as one of the most responsible young men around. If you know someone who fits this description, you may know how interesting the behavior proves to be. Even though it's learned behavior, it can also be said that some learn much better than others. For example, consider the siblings who grow up in the same household. All may have been taught to be responsible, but some are usually better at adhering to the standard than others.

What happens when the propensity for responsible behavior is combined with Christ-centered faith? It's easy to surmise that faith in Christ will enhance whatever human characteristics one possesses. However, I'm referring to the observable behavioral characteristics that can be used to describe such enhancements. Recognizing and analyzing the behaviors that characterize the synthesis of faith and responsible action enables the believer to improve relationships in ministry, in earthly relationships, and with Christ. Have you observed behavior in other people that seemed strange or, at best, contrary to your way of doing things? Even though the body of Christ is diverse, it's still possible to mismanage relationships because we lack insight into the origins of behavioral differences.

This chapter provides additional information about the faith-style that fuses stable service and evidential faith, referred to in this book as the *action faith-style.*

Faith Orientation

Christian faith was described earlier as hope, reliance, and trust in God through unwavering belief that Christ died for the remission of our sins and was resurrected on the third day. As a result, we have eternal life and all the privileges as heirs to God's kingdom. Faith is "the substance of things hoped for, the evidence of things not seen" (Heb. 11:1 KJV). A person's faith orientation consists of observable behavior patterns when dealing with uncertainties. If one's coping mechanism for handling the unknown is hope, reliance, and trust in God, based on the belief that Christ died for sinners, it's safe to conclude that Christian faith is operative. Even though Christian faith is a concept germane to all believers, the manner in which faith is applied is as individualistic as each believer's personality. Service in ministry organizations provides an isolated aspect of human experience in which the application of faith can be observed and interpreted.

People who score high in the action area of the Faith-Style Inventory are described as having responsibility-oriented faith. Responsibility is demonstrated by a strong appreciation for accountability, obligation, and duty. Believers who demonstrate responsibility-oriented faith as their dominant style seldom fail to "come through with the goods." Responsibility-oriented faith is characterized by a strong desire to "not let God down."

Evidence and stability are the pillars of the responsibility-oriented faith-style. *A person* demonstrating responsibility-oriented faith is highly concerned with providing evidence of commitment to God. The belief is that each act of faith should, in some way, produce evidence of steadfastness. In doing so, the act provides encouragement to move further and more boldly into uncertainties that may otherwise become hindrances. The demonstration of commitment through evidence is seen as increasingly pleasing to God. After all, "without faith it is impossible to please him" (Heb. 11:6).

> *Responsibility-oriented faith is characterized by a strong desire to "not let God down."*

Stability is also an essential part of responsibility-oriented faith. Faith, in accordance with this style, is shown by activities that follow a linear progression. For one of this faith-style orientation, to engage in activities that don't follow a linear progression indicates confusion and "double-mindedness." Most believers are familiar with James' description of a double-minded man who is "unstable in all he does" (James 1:8). Spontaneity isn't the strength of the responsibility-oriented faith-style. Unplanned activity is interpreted as an unnecessary distraction that diminishes productivity for the kingdom. Responsibility-oriented faith is based on certain assumptions about God and what constitutes a healthy relationship with the Lord. The assumptions are neither correct nor incorrect, but what's more important is to understand the assumptions rather than to judge whether they're valid. Examining the underlying assumptions for this style will help those who have it as their dominant style, as well as those who possess other dominant styles.

Assumption

The most fundamental, underlying assumption in responsibility-oriented faith is that faith is demonstrated by one's uncompromising commitment to action, which is the basis for real progress. Action is always executed. Even rest or contemplation is viewed as an activity that leads to a calculable result. Remaining active is the key to working with those whose faith is expressed through their accountable behavior.

I once led a group of highly talented and creative people. The members of this team were living proof that creativity doesn't usually occur in linear, structured environments. They were talkative, seemingly undisciplined, and openly engaged in activities that appeared to be frivolous, such as reading or just staring at the ceiling. Yet, their productivity measured higher than any of their peer groups. Those who possess responsibility-oriented faith-styles perceive time that's not action-intensive as unproductive, unless the activity contributes to the results in a linear fashion. If there's a scheduled time for silent reflection, there must be an objective expectation for what will be produced.

That's why, for those who demonstrate responsibility-oriented faith-style, faith without "specific" works is dead. The care taken to successfully complete tasks is an indicator of a person's belief that the task can be accomplished. Faith is made alive in the action it evokes. The evidential nature of this style says that to profess faith and then do nothing amounts to no faith at all. This may sound rigid and legalistic, but many people show faith by doing. As expressed in James 1:22, failing to "do" is self-deceiving. It's an indication that people have forgotten what they heard, or it may be concluded that they never believed at all.

Responsibility-oriented faith produces certain experiences that may be common among those with this dominant style. Focusing on the common experiences will provide a sense of "I'm not so strange after all."

Common Experiences

It's beneficial to identify some common experiences shared by those who demonstrate faith in a responsibility-oriented manner. The value of our diversity is best realized when common experiences are shared. Identifying common experiences allows others to "look through the lens" of our experience. Sharing evokes empathy and strengthens relationships.

It's not uncommon for those who score high in the responsibility-oriented faith-style to feel like, or be perceived as, the "task police" when serving with others. The desire to remain on course and follow prescribed directions is often manifested in the role of task maintenance. The extent to which responsibility-oriented believers feel isolated in this role usually determines the tenaciousness of their effort. The assumptions that undergird the thought and actions of possessors of this style are deeply rooted. Comments such as "let's get back on task," and "shouldn't we move on" are never more than a breath away from the vocal cords of the "responsible one."

The overwhelming belief that strict adherence to linear progression is the only path to productive ministry can be so frustrating that it may result in extreme anxiety if left unfulfilled.

This is why some possessors of this dominant style opt to serve alone rather than experience the frustration of continually having to "drag others along." There's nothing wrong with serving alone if the project calls for independent activity. However, in this age of evangelism teams, praise teams, ministry teams, and every other kind of team imaginable, it's unlikely that anyone will serve in isolation for long. There's simply too much interconnectivity to realistically expect complete solitude. The accelerating electronic information age has diminished opportunities to serve in isolation.

The advantage of the responsibility-oriented faith-style is that possessors usually have a reputation for completing the job and getting things accomplished, but sometimes their desire to get things done causes the sponsors of the activity to discount the importance of relationships. What have we really accomplished if we have a very productive group that brings tasks to completion, but their relationships suffer because they don't really get along? Responsibility-oriented believers feel as though they're dragging others along. People with whom they interact and who possess other styles as being dominant, feel as if they're being dragged along. The project is completed, but relationships suffer.

There's extreme value in having responsibility-oriented believers involved in any effort because they tend to demonstrate measurable results. I believe God wants us to be accountable. We should be able to demonstrate and document progress, which is consistent with the natural tendencies and desires of the responsibility-oriented believer. Personality traits make them able to demonstrate results to those who want to see evidence of measurable progress.

Personality

There's no single, accepted definition of *personality* among psychological theorists. For our purpose, I'll simply refer to *personality* as unique behavioral patterns displayed in physical, mental, and spiritual action that distinguishes one as a person. We all possess personality traits for which we're recognized, some are the result of genetics; others are learned behavior.

Personality traits consistent with the responsibility-oriented faith-style take on added significance when examined in the context of environment. Progress is largely dependent upon a person's ability to enact faith to deal with uncertainties in existing environments. Those who are highly action-focused have personalities that cause them to be more comfortable when the environments are stable, and situations don't involve a large number of variables. Responsibility-oriented personalities feel more comfort when environments are relatively stable, changing infrequently. Rapid changes create a climate in which activity evolves too quickly to satisfy the responsibility-oriented faith-style. In the same manner, situations that are limited in complexity allow the responsibility-oriented person to behave in a manner consistent with a preferred style.

The dominant tendencies in any faith-style aren't to be judged as better or worse. We all possess some traits associated with other styles. However, some traits are just more dominant in our personalities. Also, it's better to describe the styles as more or less consistent with particular environmental conditions. It's then possible to adjust our behavior based on environmental demands. For example, serving in a smaller ministry in a stable environment demands less complexity. In contrast, serving in a specific function within ministry (e.g., finance) in a rapidly growing congregation provides a much different experience. The nature of the responsibility-oriented faith-style suggests that each task must be brought to full closure before moving to or adding on new tasks. People who score high in action will have to put forth a concerted effort to exercise their less dominant styles. A person's ability to utilize a less-dominant style will depend upon the level of the dominant score and the opportunities to develop lesser traits. A score of 60 in the action area indicates the most extreme responsibility-oriented faith. It would be more difficult for one who possesses this score to consciously demonstrate traits of experiment-oriented faith than someone with an action score of 18.

Personality plays a large role in the way faith is exercised. Each faith-style has particular traits that are more prevalent. People become better rounded in their application of faith when they're able to purposefully display diverse style characteristics. Those who are able to do so are better equipped for adapting to the changing environments. Being able to recognize and understand styles enhances the ability to serve productively with others through the effective application of faith-based principles (see Table 4 for an overview of responsibility-oriented personality traits and conditional factors).

Table 4
**Responsibility-Oriented Personality Traits
and Conditional Factors**

PERSONALITY TRAIT	ENVIRONMENT	
	Simple	**Complex**
Reliable	Style Consistency	Style Contradiction
Accountable		
Goal-Oriented		
Results-Conscious		

Strengths

While the intention isn't to present one style as superior to any other, there are qualities that are common in each style that are considered strengths. For example, those who are dominant in the action area usually demonstrate the ability to stay on track. Their efforts are focused, and so is their faith. When others are deviating from the task, succumbing to distractions or losing track of the mission, the responsibility-oriented servant is able to stay the course. This brings much needed balance to groups in need of determination, and also positions the responsibility-oriented servant as the person to call upon when the mission is critical.

Staying on course isn't a function of activity alone, but also of action with a broader purpose. I've observed ministries that have lost sight of the larger mission. As a result, the ministry and the servants' activities are driven by annual days, retreats, conferences, and educational activities that have no relationship to a broader purpose. The track upon which responsibility-oriented servants advance is maintained by a mission.

The sense of mission and the desire to produce an audit trail is par for the course for responsibility-oriented ministry participants. Their attention to detail is valuable for those who are charged with keeping track of results. If there's a form to fill out, a report to write, or strict objectives to fulfill, responsibility-oriented faith enables the servant to provide a valuable part of the productivity puzzle. I noticed this recently during the implementation of a ministry project development model in the ministry where I serve. The model required ministry participants to use a tool guiding them through the complete thought process for effectively documenting the development of new or existing ministry ideas. Goals and objectives were written, scope defined, and risks identified. As the new procedures became part of the ministry culture, I observed those who were most excited about the new tool. Better still, I noticed during follow-up that there were those who implemented the process without further prodding. Responsibility-oriented faith was operative. Not only did the tool give them the structure they enjoyed, it strengthened the connection between their activities and the mission of the church.

The concerted effort of responsibility-oriented believers is valuable in any ministry effort. They provide a means of objective measurements that emerge from their task-driven view of faith. Their service is valuable in this age of faith-based initiatives. As funders seek outlets in the faith community for philanthropic endeavors, responsibility-oriented believers will be able to demonstrate measurable results and handle the administrative demands of grants management. Yet, even with all of the added value, there are limitations that must be taken into consideration.

Limitations

Limitations aren't always obvious to those who possess them. We need to always check ourselves to determine if our patterns of behavior facilitate progress or serve as a hindrance. We should aim to operate out of our strengths, while working to diminish our weaknesses.

One limitation of responsibility-oriented servants is that they're not as adaptable to change as some who possess other styles. The single-minded focus on taking action and moving the process helps in many ways, but can also become a tremendous problem. These traits work well in arenas that don't often change. However, the tendency to whole-heartedly commit can place servants in a position where they're unable or unwilling to change. Sometimes it's not an issue of defiance, but just that stopping momentum and changing direction takes a great deal of energy. Responsibility-oriented servants shouldn't allow their single-minded focus to keep them from acknowledging the demand for flexibility. It's very unlikely that any project will proceed from beginning to end without the need for a change in direction.

Responsibility-oriented faith practices have the potential of limiting creativity when the style is practiced from a control perspective. Control always stifles creativity. It's possible to relinquish control, expect accountability, and sustain creativity simultaneously. But, it requires an awareness of faith-styles.

Diversion frustrates responsibility-oriented people. While members of other style clusters can shift attention, responsibility-oriented servants move with deliberate intent that can only be attributed to the belief in who God is and what God does, and the gift of faith. Anything that deviates from the norm or disturbs their concentration is a diversion. The eagerness to avoid deviations can cause valuable information to be lost.

Summary

Responsibility-oriented faith is characterized by a complete commitment to action. Responsibility-oriented believers see activity as a way of pleasing God. They believe activity leads to progress, which is pleasing to God. They find themselves more engaged in the implementation phase of ministry projects than the planning stage. Their preoccupation with concrete measures doesn't generate appeal for conceptual activities. Faith drives their action-oriented behavior even when the end results are shrouded in uncertainty.

Interactions with others can be a source of frustration for responsibility-oriented believers. Their tendency to take on the role of "activity police" can be frustrating for them, as well as the people who work with them. Sometimes they end up serving alone because they become overly frustrated when attempting to inspire people to their same level of concern for action. This isn't necessarily a negative tendency. Role identity and clarification takes on added importance. The ministry advances and the participants are more fulfilled when they serve in capacities consistent with their particular faith-style. The reputation of responsibility-oriented servants for getting the job done suggests they have a strategic role to play in any ministry organization. The challenge is getting them involved in the appropriate activities, performing the most appropriate function.

The ability of responsibility-oriented people to show results is unparalleled. Regardless of the ministry size, the ability of showing measurable progress is important. It enables those who are given charge of the ministry to manage their responsibilities in a manner that affirms accountability, helping them to stay on task. When those with a more experimental nature are drifting into realms outside the original vision, the responsibility-oriented believer gets everyone "back on track."

But there are cautions. The same qualities that make the action faith-style one of responsibility, also presents potential problems. We live in an age of continuous and rapid change. Ministries must respond to the environment while maintaining the original mission of the church. Those with action faith-styles have difficulty adapting to change. Their focus on getting things done doesn't allow for the deviations that unexpected change can bring, and their creativity is limited by their unwillingness to "get off track." They would be very content to do the same things everyday for a long time. Their steadfastness can often provide much needed stability when ministries experience inevitable volatility.

Discussion Guide

1.   What role does responsibility play in your relationship with God?

2.   Have you ever served on a ministry project with a responsibility-oriented believer? If so, discuss this experience.

3.   Do you prefer to work alone or on ministry teams? Why?

4.   What are three ways people with action faith-style can improve on their ability to be flexible?

5.   If you were working on a ministry project team, would you prefer to have more responsibility-oriented believers on the team than other faith-styles? Why or why not?

CHAPTER 10

Understanding Faith-Inspired Vision

S ome people can see themselves and their activities in a futuristic manner. I often observe this quality in some of the more successful pastors in the country. They have the ability to see the manifestation of purpose at a time when others only see the reality of current conditions. Their ability to see potential in the context of purpose enables them to build and sustain momentum progressively, even in the face of adversity. Faith is the foundation of their vision. The people they lead and the projects they facilitate are the beneficiaries of their ability to see with transcendent vision.

The same is true not only for great pastors, but for all visionaries. When their ability to see is combined with other essential personality traits, they often become known as great leaders. Their ability to cast and communicate vision makes the future seem more attainable for others who aspire to move forward. Just think of the countless people who exhibit this quality: parents, teachers, friends, and others encountered along your journey.

What does this quality mean when it's inspired by Christian faith? This chapter will help to examine faith-inspired vision as described in the Servant Resource Faith-Style Model and Inventory. You will gain insight enabling you to better understand your actions, as well as the actions of those with whom you serve or interact. Greater understanding will lead to more focused acts of faith.

Faith Orientation

Purposeful faith is described as vision-oriented, the ability to see beyond the present. Divine purpose is linked to a person's ability to see or comprehend a future application. The ability to "see" is understood by using the analogy of great visual artists. Many painters, sculptors, and others who engage in such craft are able to "see" the end product before it's achieved. If you asked how they knew a piece of art was finished, they would explain: "I knew it was finished, because that's how I envisioned it." The product was only visible in their mind. When such an ability to see is combined with divine purpose born of Christian faith, the vision takes on a completely different significance.

As indicated by the Servant Resource Faith-Style Model, purposeful, vision-oriented faith is based on expectancy that the vision can be achieved. The expectancy is heightened by the belief that fulfillment of the vision is consistent with God's will and purpose. There may be very little evidence to support fulfillment of the vision, yet there's a great deal of faith-driven expectation.

Such faith is an essential element on ministry teams. Those who serve in ministry are often called upon to create a lot with very little. I saw this kind of faith in action recently. It wasn't operative on a ministry team, but in the behavior of a person who is the president of a small college in the heart of a large urban center. The college is a state institution, but its leader isn't shy in his expressions of faith. He plainly displays a Bible in the confines of his office and calls for prayer prior to meals. It's clear to me and all who encounter him that he's comfortable letting people know the importance of his faith in Christ.

I've watched the school struggle financially and go through many periods of hardship. Yet, the undercurrent of faith remains. Constituents are inspired by their leader's ability to see a bright future in spite of current circumstances. The school's mission, which is to serve students from urban high schools who don't fit the profile of the typical 18- to 22-year-old college student, is consistent with his Christian values about helping those who face challenges. Many of the students are young, single parents who work full-time, attend college full-time, and cope with the demands of parenting. However, the president perceives a connection between God's purpose for his life and his vision of empowering people to overcome adversity through education. Like the artist, he's able to see those who face obstacles in a future state of success and achievement. The college wouldn't be the same without his faith, as well as his sense of mission and vision.

There are many implications for ministry teams as related to vision-oriented faith. The tendency for them to have an unwavering expectancy for fulfillment of God's purpose can be the catalyst leading the team through difficulties. The style also leads to stability in service. Maintaining focus regarding purpose and vision contributes to long-term steadiness of direction. We have all experienced ministry efforts that errantly go beyond the scope of vision or simply lose direction. The presence of vision-oriented believers helps to maintain direction and keep ministry projects on track. Their steadfastness enables them to make welcomed contributions, even though their style may be contrary to others on the team. A high-performing team always has diversity of style, thought, and approach. The vision is indeed for an appointed time (Hab. 2:3). Vision-oriented believers help us to be attentive until that time arrives.

Assumption

The purposeful faith-style is based on certain assumptions. People who exhibit a strong sense of divine purpose do so in accordance with their views about who God is and what God does, and about the gift of faith. They believe that properly applied faith leads to the realization of a specific vision. Visions are likely to be achieved in a progressive manner, just as they were originally conceived. Vision-oriented servants also believe that faith can be used as a tool for achieving exact, distinct objectives with surgical precision. Vision is seen as an instrument of divine communication. The will of God is revealed holistically or gradually in a manner that enables the recipient to work toward the fulfillment of the vision.

Vision, or revealed purpose, is the disclosure of what was unknown. The efficacy of vision rests on the believer's acceptance of God's ability to provide guidance. There's an understanding that such vision will always lead to an encounter with divine purpose. Where would we be without such a belief? Ministry would be pointless because of the lack of connection between revelation and the will of God.

I have witnessed this phenomenon in people who work in secular organizations but fail to make the connection between their services in the company and God's purpose for their lives. Service without purpose is unfulfilling and empty. Personal fulfillment is directly proportional to one's sense of mission and purpose. Millions of people are beset by job dissatisfaction because of their lack of purpose. Lack of purpose can lead to what's commonly called "going through the motions" until the situation becomes unbearable. Tragically, many people don't realize what's actually missing from their experience. They leave the position often blaming the organization, only to repeat the same cycle of dissatisfaction and disillusionment in another situation.

The assumption on which this faith-style is developed remains critical to the success of any ministry effort. It's essential that ministry leaders work diligently to help ministry participants develop the type of faith that reinforces the understanding that God provides guidance. As long as we sincerely desire to see divine will come to pass, God will reveal the unknown and bring us soundly into the fulfillment of our destiny.

There's also an inherent assumption that we will be able to gauge whether we're continuing to move in accordance with God's will. Continuous, or at least periodic, assessments are necessary to determine if our actions are consistent with God's desires. We can achieve this by evaluating progress in contrast to the original vision, or by determining whether God's original intent has changed. I believe that God will alter plans pertaining to methodology. However, God's ultimate desire never changes—for "all men to be saved and to come to the knowledge of the truth" (1 Tim. 2:4).

Divine revelation is always consistent with the goal of helping people accept Christ as Savior and Lord, and gives meaning to vision-oriented faith. Vision-oriented believers' ability to move beyond difficulties and obstacles is predicated on a sense that God provides the light that illuminates their path. They're not overly concerned with the territory beyond the light. There's a sincere belief that God's light is more than capable of penetrating any darkness and uncovering any pitfall. As a result, the will of God is fulfilled and God is glorified through the application of their faith.

Common Experiences

Vision-oriented servants are seen as "big-picture" people, effective at developing strategy because they keep the end in mind. They're also able to easily see the scope of whatever project they become involved in, which is an ability not easy for everybody. Some people are consumed by details, which become so overwhelming that they lose sight of the overall mission. This loss becomes obvious when you hear people ask questions like, "Why are we here anyway?" In reflection, the question sounds a bit comical, but we've all been involved in projects where that question is valid.

Big-picture people don't always have to be in official leadership roles; however, we always need them. They can wield positive influence regardless of their responsibility. Their ability to refocus by requesting a pause in the process is invaluable. They seem to know exactly the right time to ask everyone to "step back" and take a fresh look at the situation. Their official role is inconsequential, especially if the process is designed to be team-oriented. When team participants establish themselves as persons of vision-oriented faith, other team members defer to their judgment regarding big-picture issues. People tend to listen when a person operates from a confident posture, which often emerges when acting in one's dominant style. Even if others don't see the big picture immediately, it takes

Vision-oriented servants are seen as "big-picture" people, effective at developing strategy because they keep the end in mind.

only a few experiences to convince them that they need someone with broad vision to help them stay on course. Conversely, too many visionaries can cause failure. Who is going to take care of the details if everyone is surveying the big picture? Details bore vision-oriented believers.

One common complaint about those who demonstrate vision-oriented faith is they act prematurely. This may not be a valid complaint considering such believers often see what others don't. It's not uncommon for them to be perceived as "pushy" or domineering simply because they're acting in accordance with their vision. People of vision-oriented faith learn skills that enable them to communicate and act with patience. They learn to keep the vision before their partners while not dragging them in a direction they're not ready for. Momentum increases as others

People of vision-oriented faith . . .
learn to keep the vision before their partners
while not dragging them in a direction
they're not ready for.

begin to adopt the vision. No formula guarantees that everyone will adopt the vision of the purposeful believer. There's also no way to govern completely the speed with which people accept the visionary's view. The only method of promoting the vision is to develop relationship skills for easing the anxieties of the more resistant participants.

Periods of accelerating change present a particular problem for people with vision-oriented faith. Rapid change may engender out-of-control feelings because fulfilled purpose is predicated on a sense of completion and closure. Periods of rapid change make it more difficult to achieve the closure which is vital for purpose fulfillment, thus the importance of overall purpose. Many frustrated ministry servants express a sense of "moving too fast." They wonder why the ministry is involved in so many endeavors simultaneously, failing to realize the ministry must respond to the environment to remain relevant and vibrant. Show me a ministry whose internal complexity doesn't mirror the complexity of the environment, and I'll show you a ministry on the decline. Those who operate in a vision-oriented faith-style must always take their beliefs to the largest common denominator to remain fluid: All must be saved and come to the knowledge of truth.

Personality

Vision-oriented servants demonstrate unique behavior patterns. Their tendency to be focused causes certain behaviors to emerge, influencing their relationships and the way they serve. They can be described as single-mindedly determined, unwavering in their resolve to see that objectives are met. As such, simple environments are more comfortable for those who demonstrate vision-oriented faith. It's easier to focus on objective outcomes when the environment isn't continuously accelerating. Simple environments enable vision-oriented servants to avoid adjusting the vision as frequently as they would if the environment was more volatile.

The personality accompanying the vision-oriented faith-style is also more comfortable with simple, rather than complex, environments. Rapid change presents one type of difficulty, which is compounded if filled with a multitude of variables and situations. Complex environments present a similar dilemma. The more variables present, the more difficult it is for the vision-oriented servant to maintain the necessary focus. Awareness of personality tendencies will help visionaries become more effective in ministry.

I sometimes reflect on the differences in the ministry where I now serve and the ministry of my youth. The church of my youth was a small ministry in a rural setting during the 1960s and 1970s. The amount of change that we experienced from one year to the next was negligible. Each year brought about the usual annual celebrations, such as Christmas and Easter programs, church anniversary, and picnics. Such things as the Internet, television ministry, and multiple services on Sunday morning weren't part of our experience. In fact, the ministry still functions today as it did 35 years ago. The declining population in this area is probably the most significant environmental change. What a contrast to where I now minister, serving more than 7,000 congregants in a major metropolitan area, with three Sunday morning worship services, a burgeoning national television ministry, a vibrant Internet presence, and all of the administrative, technological, and financial systems required for such endeavors. In the environment of my youth, refocusing vision to respond to a rapidly evolving environment wasn't a concern. The personality that's comfortable in simple and less complex conditions would be very satisfied in the ministry of my early development. Vision-inspired faith-styles are often perceived as prudent and confident (see Table 5, "Vision-Oriented Personality Traits and Conditional Factors"). The methodical way vision-oriented servants approach their ministry assignments is admired by some colleagues and disliked by others. Their systematic approach gives the perception of surety. Ministry team members also benefit from the attention to detail and process. However, the care they demonstrate is sometimes viewed as too time consuming and unreceptive to innovation. While linear thinkers appreciate their strict attention to process, others see structured process as too restrictive. The belief that faith leads to the realization of specific vision contributes to the assurance that's such a dominant part of the purposeful servant's personality.

Table 5
**Vision-Oriented Personality Traits
and Conditional Factors**

PERSONALITY TRAIT	ENVIRONMENT	
	Simple	**Complex**
Focused	Style Consistency	Style Contradiction
Intentional		
Prudent		
Confident		

Strengths

Groups and teams are subject to collective thought patterns. Our strengths help improve the collective experience of all ministry partners. Strengths become part of the blend that determines the effectiveness and efficiency of the ministry team. Synergy, the ability of participants to reap collective results that surpass their individual contributions, is born out of the deployment strengths within the team. When vision-oriented faith is interjected in a group experience, it provides a sense of mission that's critical to the development of synergy. Ministry team strength is often manifested in the form of strong mission and purpose.

The primary strength of vision-oriented servants is their ability to maintain sight of the "why" of any service endeavor. This is important to the individual servant, as well as to the effort of ministry team members. For the individual servant, the ability to focus on the "why" offers a sense of direction, which allows them to avoid the pitfall of frustration and disappointment that can paralyze the progress of even

The primary strength of vision-oriented servants is their ability to maintain sight of the "why" of any service endeavor.

the most well-intentioned servant. The sense of direction possessed by the vision-oriented servants can be a positive influence on all who share their endeavors. They're able to provide a sense of reason for activities that otherwise seem to have no purpose. Ministry teams often need someone to focus everyone's consciousness on the reason for existence, which is often ignored. Keeping the ministry team purpose-conscious energizes the team.

Limitations

Matthew 28:19-20, known as The Great Commission, details the ultimate mission of ministry service: We live, move, and act to make disciples and teach them to obey the precepts of Jesus. However, there are certain concerns that must be considered as we seek to execute service with vision-oriented faith. A dominant vision-oriented style may cause servants to lose sight of God's "equifinality,"[1] the ability to bring about the same results in a multitude of ways. Reaffirming the equifinality of God enables those with vision-oriented faith-styles to avoid being overwhelmed by their tendency to seek linear paths. There are numerous ways to accomplish the same results. The will and purpose of God may encompass any of those directions. Failure to recognize the variety in God's approach causes us to be too restrictive when serving. There's a point at which vision-oriented faith hinders the way ministry projects evolve and the way change occurs. If we become blindly committed to purpose, we fail to acknowledge many changes that are inevitable and necessary to remain vibrant. The mission of ministry will always be the same, but methods will continually evolve.

People with vision-oriented faith are easily frustrated when others don't adopt their vision. The best way to overcome this potential pitfall is for people who possess the purposeful style to always assume the role of servant-teacher. The role of servant-teacher can be incorporated into the scope of any project or purpose. Servant-teachers don't find it burdensome to coach others into adopting their vision. In fact, the teacher role becomes pleasurable because it's seen as progress toward the vision. Servant-teachers also approach the instructional moment from a different perspective than those who simply teach. Servant-teachers instruct with an emphasis on providing the learner with information required to fulfill the learning objective. We can never exclude the role of servant-teacher, for it alleviates problems that can emerge when others don't adopt the vision.

Summary

Faith-inspired vision is the ability to see future accomplishments in spite of current circumstances. It's the ability of the mind to picture the completion of service endeavors that fulfill the purpose of God. Such visions are the foundation of the purposeful faith-style. Divine purpose is directly associated with a person's ability to envision how the purpose relates to future activity. Those with vision-oriented faith are stable in their approach to service and filled with belief expectancy. Purposeful believers make valuable contributions to ministry teams because of their ability to stay focused, helping to propel the team past difficulties while fulfilling purpose.

Vision-oriented servants assume they can fulfill vision as it was originally revealed to them through the diligent application of faith. Sincere pursuit of purpose facilitates divine revelation about bringing the vision to fruition. Consistency with divine purpose is measured by progress in fulfilling the vision as originally revealed to them. In the grand scheme, divine purpose is that all people be saved and come to the knowledge of the truth. All visions revealed to purposeful servants will be consistent with this ultimate desire of God.

The nature of vision-oriented faith sets the stage for common experiences among those who possess this faith-style as their dominant style. They're usually the ones who see and communicate the "big picture" and are welcomed members on any ministry team, except when there are too many visionaries on the same team. They also are sometimes accused of acting prematurely. Their ability to see the final results before others causes them to take steps that others aren't ready to take.

Vision-oriented servants demonstrate particular personality traits. They're more comfortable when the environment is simple. Too many variables distract them from linear progress toward fulfilling their purpose, progress that is usually perceived as prudent behavior.

There are strengths and limitations also associated with the vision-oriented faith-style. Vision-oriented servants are able to maintain sight of why they're engaged in each ministry effort, with diversions not being a problem. Their ability to maintain focus brings surety to any ministry team on which they serve. Contrarily, they also tend to be restrictive when it comes to seeking purpose. Their narrow scope leaves little room for shifts in vision fulfillment. Shifts in method seem to unsettle the surety they thrive on, and they tend to become frustrated when others are slow to adopt their vision.

Vision-oriented faith is a productive tool when accompanied by awareness on the part of those who utilize it. Awareness enables visionaries to serve effectively and make valuable contributions to ministry efforts that might otherwise be lost. They're the embodiment of what it means to "cast the vision and make it plain" (Hab. 2:2 KJV).

Discussion Guide

1. Discuss the positive experiences you've had with those who demonstrate vision-oriented faith.

2. What strategies can be employed to offset some of the limitations of the vision-oriented faith?

3. Would you describe the environment in which you serve as simple or complex? What adjustments will you make to help other purposeful servants, or yourself, make a more significant contribution to ministry efforts?

4. What percentage of the current ministry team on which you serve consists of people who demonstrate a dominant purposeful faith-style?

5. What adjustments will you make if there's a large number of purposeful servants on your ministry team? What adjustments will you make if there are few or none?

CHAPTER 11

Understanding Faith-Inspired Experimentation

T he creative faith-style is experiment-oriented. Those who demonstrate experiment-oriented faith are more inclined to test "uncharted waters." In the strictest sense, experimentation refers to activity for the purpose of discovering something or showing something to be true. Incorporating this concept with one's faith implies that experimentation isn't done just for the sake of testing an idea or theory, but is done as an undertaking that has a foundation in a belief system. Experiment-oriented faith doesn't suggest that particular outcomes are expected. However, it inspires people to act in an unrestricted quest to glorify God.

A predetermined path has a great deal less significance for those who are highly experiment-oriented than it does for others. Those who are more responsibility- and vision-oriented take predetermined guidelines more seriously. Experimenters often operate outside the boundaries of predetermined plans. While it may seem reckless to some, the results often justify the tendency not to act in accordance with the script.

Understanding others and ourselves in the context of experiment-oriented faith enables us to position ourselves for greater spiritual growth and to more effectively serve with others. Ministry teams will be stronger and our contributions to teams enhanced. The creative faith-style is my favorite because it's fun and spontaneous, and it focuses on newness. This style enables us to bring life to our service and go beyond limited capabilities and expectations.

Faith Orientation

Like the vision-oriented faith, experiment-oriented faith is based on an expectation about the future. A penchant for experimentation is carried out with a belief that a desired result will emerge during the rendering of service. Expectation gives those who possess this style as dominant the freedom to improvise. I liken them to talented musicians who know how to read music, but enjoy improvisation. The next note is never predictable, yet sounds great. They can play the same song multiple times, and it never sounds exactly the same.

Experiment-oriented faith is based on a person's belief in the omnipotence and sovereignty of God. The basis of faith is stated in Luke 1:37, "For nothing is impossible with God." This brief statement expresses God's limitless ability. When faith is anchored by such belief, expectation of the eventual manifestation of God's will drives people's resolve to continue trying. Their faith suggests to them that service isn't always rendered with a preconceived result. God is creating even as we serve, and the end product may be totally unlike what was envisioned at the beginning of the process. Nonetheless, the result is to God's glory and often exceeds our preconceived notions.

I can't even count the number of times I have undertaken a ministry project with a picture of what the end result would be, only to be surprised by what ultimately emerged. This doesn't discount the necessity for planning. Instead it means that all plans are subject to revision as we allow God to intervene and guide our efforts. The degree to which experiment-oriented faith is dominant determines how easily a person is willing to submit to what feels like God's improvisation. Even though God is omniscient and fully knows what the end will be, we often experience divine movements as unrehearsed because they don't exactly fit our ideas. The more we're willing to allow God to guide the brush as it crosses the canvas of our experiences, the more we benefit from the Lord's creative power.

Experiment-oriented faith relies on open-ended hope and confident desire. The hope is open-ended in the respect that God's will is what a person ultimately wants. There's confidence in this desire based on the understanding of what God can do. In the spiritual gift mix of many successful pastors, strong faith is usually present along with a strong creative faith-style. Consider some of the more successful ministries around the country in terms of their effectiveness. Many of the leaders demonstrate an ability to go with God, meaning they're able to discern opportunities and move swiftly toward them

Experiment-oriented faith relies on open-ended hope and confident desire.

with confidence. Their confidence holds fast even when the picture doesn't materialize as imagined. Their belief that God is creating something beautiful and unique inspires others to move into the opportunity with less concern about the apparent uncertainty. Whether it's a new ministry, community project, or order of Sunday morning worship, experiment-oriented faith has a great impact on followers.

Faith is the substance of our hope. What didn't previously exist can emerge in a way that's directly proportional to our ability to believe. Experimentation should be encouraged in ministry efforts, not in an irresponsible manner but in a way that doesn't put limitations on our ability to participate in creative activity with God. Even though limited by the constraints of human characteristics, we serve a God who is sovereign (Ps. 115:3).

Assumption

A correlation exists between the closeness of people's relationship with God and their behavior. The influence of close relationships can't be denied. I need only to examine my relationship with my earthly father to confirm this reality. We all have learned behaviors that we aren't aware of as a result of our relationship with our parents. Regardless of whether the adopted characteristics are perceived as positive, the influence is inevitable. How often have you observed personal qualities that you can only attribute to the influence of your parents? We look into the mirror of time daily saying, "I'm turning into my parents."

The assumption that is the foundation of the experiment-oriented faith is that we're made in God's image. Therefore, we have innovative capacity that's generated from our reliance on God. We're God's children and can't avoid demonstrating characteristics that are part of God's nature. My earthly father is a retired school principal and education was always emphasized in our home. He's also very good with his hands, single-handedly building a gorgeous home that was more than adequate to accommodate the seven children who were reared there. The two garages, patios, landscaping, and other amenities are unparalleled and still the pride of the community. He would often contract himself out in the community during the summer months when school was closed. It was a good source of secondary income, but I believe he also just enjoyed the work.

As much as I tried to avoid adopting his passion for construction, I didn't have much of a choice. He would hire my friends and me to work with him during the summer. Needless to say, I didn't necessarily enjoy the work. Yet, to this day, I can still mix concrete, lay bricks, lay a foundation, install cabinets, repair plumbing, and execute any number of handy procedures. We can never be sure which of our parents' characteristics will emerge in our personality or behavior, but we can say with assurance that something will surface. In the case of experiment-oriented faith, creativity is a dominant characteristic in the way faith is exercised.

We're all creative. Some of us are more comfortable with our creativity and don't mind the experimentation that's involved. Yet, the fact remains that the creative capacity is part of our spiritual composition. The relationship we enjoy with God makes the creative capacity an inevitable personal characteristic. Just think of the power that would be unleashed if we fully accepted and began to operate in the assurance of that reality. Tapping into our innate ability to bring about newness would help us to avoid stagnation, which we all too often struggle to overcome. Ministries that are beset by routine and the lack of innovation must seek to identify and empower the creative capacities resident in their congregations. Miracles occur when experiment-oriented faith is united with God's mission and vision. A breath of new life flows into the ministry because the assumption of relationship and influence is operative.

I'm grateful to my parents for what they were able to pass on to me. Now that I'm more mature, I take great delight in the fact that I have the ability to do home improvements, even if I don't have the time. But I'm more grateful for what God has passed on to me. We're able to break the bonds of routine and remain relevant in an ever-changing world because of our relationship with God and the power of God's influence. I'm also grateful that the relationship has no limitations. My ability to utilize creative capacity is only limited by my ability to believe. The creativity that's born of our relationship can continually be explored so we might be more effective and productive in our faith.

Common Experiences

Certain experiences are common to those who demonstrate creativity in their faith. Their view of the world and their understanding of who God is and what God can do cause them to see events from a similar point of view. There are also similarities in the way they're perceived, which is often as "over the edge," excessive, or unpredictable. While this is indeed a perception from another's point of view, there's some basis for this perception. People who are experiment-oriented in their faith operate beyond recognized boundaries. The more people on a ministry team who possess the experiment-oriented faith as dominant, the more the team will operate beyond the boundaries.

Interesting scenarios arise when experiment-oriented people dominate a ministry team, especially if the pastor is achievement- or vision-oriented. The team is constantly seen as "out of control," a group of "loose cannons," when in reality they're simply a group that's dominated by people who exercise experiment-oriented faith. The team members experience frustration as they're constantly instructed to adhere to the guidelines. The pastor is frustrated by what he perceives to be ministry servants who simply

> *The more people on a ministry team who possess the experiment-oriented faith as dominant, the more the team will operate beyond the boundaries.*

don't want to follow instructions. The answer to the dilemma lies in careful two-way communication and the coaching skills of the pastor to harness the team's potential.

Scarce resources seemingly don't concern those who are experiment-oriented as much as it concerns others. Experiment-oriented servants find such situations to be perfect for exercising their ability to believe and create. They don't mind being "out on a limb" with God. Faith and creativity allows them to approach such situations innovatively without their efforts being constrained by overwhelming fear. We all know there are situations in which expected resources fail to materialize. Success is often determined by what happens after the initial shock of realizing that resources aren't available. It's not that creative servants don't experience the initial shock, but their ability to move beyond is based on the fact that they don't get stuck there. They're able to experience the normal emotional response and allow their faith to unleash their innovative abilities.

It's important for all people to understand how they exercise faith. Experiment-oriented servants are helped when their uniqueness is validated, and others get beyond the often-expressed perception that they're the "weird" ones. The more the experiment-oriented servants become comfortable with their unique contribution, the better their integration with the ministry. The goal isn't to separate and isolate people according to their faith-styles, but to generate greater awareness so that ministry can function more effectively as an integrated whole.

Excitement occurs when experiment-oriented faith operates. Concern for results is never ignored. However, experiment-oriented faith makes the journey so exciting that results almost become secondary. Something miraculous happens when faith-based experimentation is employed. The results often exceed expectation even when the results weren't the primary focus. I can't emphasize enough that I'm not advocating abandonment of goals, objectives, and results-oriented ministry. I'm simply saying that the unpredictable, spontaneous, "outside the box" creative style is so exciting that results seem to take care of themselves. When creative servants are at work, hold on to your hats: "No eye has seen, no ear has heard, no mind has conceived what God has prepared for those who love him" (1 Cor. 2:9).

Personality

The dominant personality traits resident in the experiment-oriented faith are no surprise. Innovative faith expressions are consistent with realities of a complex environment. The more variables present, the more opportunities people have to exercise their innovative tendencies. That's why those who possess dominant experiment-oriented faith find more satisfaction in ministries and with ministry projects that offer multiple tasks, multiple demands, and accelerated time lines. The complexity is consistent with the person's experimental nature. Stable environments and routine quickly become boring.

Characteristics that have been mentioned may lead to the idea that experiment-oriented faith involves thoughtless risk taking. That's not true. There's nothing irresponsible in the faith patterns of experiment-oriented servants. Their position remains deeply grounded in their understanding of who God is and what God can do. Their calculations aren't based on finite limitations. They fully consider their circumstances and act in accordance with their beliefs. Even if we describe their faith as blind, we have to submit that their other senses are spiritually attuned. Their actions are based on their projections about results. Experiment-oriented faith often depends on a person's ability to feel his or her way around until finding the path God desires. The destination may not be totally clear, but the process of feeling one's way around is methodical and calculated. Everyone should be able to identify with the idea of feeling one's way around until God's will is found. This is an activity that's readily accepted by the experiment-oriented servant.

The unconventional nature of experiment-oriented faith is also consistent with complexity. The personality mirrors the environment, giving it the qualities required to respond to the environment. Those with more stable faith-styles sometimes experience difficulty when attempting to respond to complex situations. Unconventional situations demand unconventional faith (see Table 6, "Experiment-Oriented Personality Traits and Conditional Factors"). I again want to emphasize the necessity for balance when serving on ministry teams. Teams may encounter a variety of environments as they seek to serve. Environments that teams serve in are subject to change. The extent to which a variety of faith-styles reside on the team enhances the team's ability to take on different types of projects in a multitude of settings successfully. The free-spirited, unconventional nature of experiment-oriented faith helps the team meet complex environment challenges. Purpose and action faith-styles help the team address the more stable service demands, "Now the body is not made up of one part but of many" (1 Cor. 12: 14).

Table 6
**Experiment-Oriented Personality Traits
and Conditional Factors**

PERSONALITY TRAIT	ENVIRONMENT	
	Simple	Complex
Innovative	Style Contradiction	Style Consistency
Calculated Risk-Taker		
Free-spirited		
Unconventional		

Strengths

The advantages of experiment-oriented faith can be gleaned from previous descriptions. It infuses new life into individual servants and ministry teams, taking them beyond their normal capabilities. The style enables people to operate without being overly concerned about resources, which is advantageous in rapidly changing environments. Yet the impact is lost if the style isn't exercised.

The strengths of this or any style are lost if they're never realized and applied. Failure to exploit the strengths occurs for various reasons. A person can simply be unaware he or she possesses the dominant tendencies and only experience the benefits sporadically, missing many of the style benefits which can be intentionally applied and enjoyed. People may

. . . experiment-oriented faith . . . infuses new life into individual servants and ministry teams . . .

be part of a ministry group that fails to identify and take advantage of the style resident in the group. There may even be awareness of the experimental style, yet failure still occurs because more stable or evidential styles are so dominant that the experiment-oriented style is overwhelmed and suppressed.

The best way to avoid losing the benefits of any faith-style is to generate awareness. Servants must develop self-awareness about their styles and how the styles influence faith and service. Ministry teams must receive training in how to manage style diversity. Greater awareness unleashes the power of faith and helps servants to fulfill their potential. The advantages will permeate the ministry organization and strengthen its ability to fulfill its mission and vision.

Limitations

Limitations surround each faith-style, which means there are certain circumstances for which the styles may be less suited. The tendency to appear aimless is one such pattern that may emerge. This may not feel uncomfortable for the person who demonstrates experiment-oriented faith. The limitation becomes apparent when the social stimulus value is taken into consideration. Whether real or perceived, aimlessness will negatively influence others, especially when the one perceived as aimless is in a leadership role. Teams may lose trust if the leadership appears to have no direction or sense of purpose. I also have to emphasize the word *appearance*. Those who possess experiment-oriented faith may have a very keen sense of direction and purpose. It's just that their tendency to not take linear paths to achieve the purpose may create the illusion of not having direction. Experiment-oriented servants who are in leadership must work harder to communicate vision to those with whom they serve. This helps to counter the perception that they're wandering.

Experimentation takes time. Responsibility- and vision-oriented servants are more time-conscious than those with experiment-oriented faith. Experimentation can contribute to drifting project timelines. It's not that experimentation should be discouraged, but rather encouraged with a concern for existing schedules. There's also value in setting up ministry teams that are exclusively for the purpose of exploring new ideas, enabling the ministry to have the benefit of experimentation and the newness that's generated. It also gives the experiment-oriented servants a place to serve where they can feel uninhibited.

Some solutions to style limitations are a matter of structure. Experiment-oriented servants don't like rigid structure. However, structure can be created that better accommodates their style. Once again, the key is balance. Balance and style diversity, combined with the appropriate structure and organization, can provide an environment that minimizes the limitations inherent in any faith-style.

Summary

Faith-inspired experimentation can lead to results beyond imagination. Marching faithfully into unfamiliar territory triggers God's transcendent power and produces what is miraculous, according to more conventional or conservative expectations. Experiment-oriented faith is born from the expectation of what isn't yet visible. Even though the end result is unrealized, the expectation clearly declares that it will emerge and its uniqueness will be representative of faith's power. Experiment-oriented faith depends upon open-ended hope and confident desire.

We're made in God's image, therefore we have creative capacity generated from our reliance on God. Creativity in faith is a product of experimentation, our willingness to explore what hasn't been tried. This behavior harmonizes with God's creative nature. Since God is the supreme Creator, we're enabled to utilize what God provides to bring about newness. God's creative capacity is part of our being.

We have to be aware of the experiences that are common among experiment-oriented servants. Awareness of the experiences enables them to be integrated into ministry teams effectively. It also helps them to personally overcome potential inhibitors by learning to vacillate between dominant and secondary styles. That they may be perceived as "loose cannons" can be minimized if they take appropriate measures to offset this perception. Their tendency to be unconcerned with time or resources is also a common experience that creative servants must be aware of and take steps to mitigate the potential negative effect.

Experiment-oriented faith is associated with certain personality traits, patterns of behavior that can be expected based on psychological composition. Experiment-oriented servants are innovative, free-spirited, unconventional people who are eager to take calculated risks. The personality traits seem to flourish with more comfort in certain environments. The more complex and rapidly changing the environment, the more comfortable the experiment-oriented servant seems to be.

Strength is realized in the social stimulus value of experiment-oriented people. The style seems to energize and bring life to the teams on which it resides. Experiment-oriented faith constantly expands the life cycle of the team, pushing it into ever-evolving experiences that extend its life and enhance productivity. New ideas emerge when experiment-oriented faith operates. Any limitations associated with this style can be overcome through self-awareness and communication. Specific consideration must be given to which roles experiment-oriented servants fill. The perception that they're wanderers may create problems when they serve in leadership roles. Balance must be maintained on teams to get maximum benefit from diversity.

Discussion Guide

1. Give examples of your creative capacity and how faith encourages your creativity.

2. Discuss a situation in which you found yourself "out on a limb" with God as you attempted to serve. How did you get there? How did the situation end? What advice would you give others who find themselves in similar circumstances?

3. List ways that your creative style has a positive influence on your ministry teams.

4. Identify a ministry project on which you're currently working. List five experiment-oriented ideas that will further your mission or the mission of your team.

5. List strategies that will help experiment-oriented leaders establish direction for those they lead.

CHAPTER 12

Understanding Faith-Inspired Achievement

Doing more, accomplishing more, having a greater impact in the community are the desires of achievement-oriented servants. Their ability to tirelessly pursue new goals is amazing, for it seems the word *rest* is absent from their vocabulary. Even if they manage to take a break, it has definite limits, and they're raring to go when the respite ends. You wonder, "When do they achieve enough?" The answer comes easily for the faithful achiever, "Enough is an unattainable quest. There are always souls to win, programs to develop, ministries to start, and classes to initiate. Growth brings about achievement, and growth should never end."

This chapter will help to bring about a deeper understanding of growth in the context of the Servant Resource Faith-Style Model (see chapter 8 and appendices 1, 2, and 3). The growth faith-style is described as achievement-oriented. On an individual level, as well as a group level, achievement-oriented faith has significant implications. Greater understanding will enable people to harness and appropriate the positive aspects of this faith-style more effectively, while minimizing the potential pitfalls associated with it. Ministry teams will be better able to manage the internal and inter-team competition, which sometimes arises when achievement-oriented faith is operative. This chapter will also help servants gain a better understanding of qualitative growth. Achieving greater quality is as positive as achieving greater quantity. Greater quantity without increases in effectiveness can lead to disaster. Faith-inspired achievement will lead to greater ministry effectiveness in most cases.

Faith Orientation

Achievement! Achievement! Achievement! Achievement-oriented faith is the evidence of what we can't see. Evidence implies there's retrievable data leading to a particular conclusion. However, in this case, the evidence is simply a belief, something accepted as truth. The belief is the only evidence required.

We sometimes underestimate the power of achievement-oriented faith. I have seen so many people overcome tremendous obstacles with achievement-oriented faith. My time on college campuses has taught me the power of achievement-oriented belief. The school where I spend a great deal of time has a significant number of students who are physically challenged, and the determination displayed by one such student will inspire me for years to come. I watched her for several years before actually having an opportunity to meet her. Despite confinement to a motorized wheelchair, she manages to make her way through the crowded corridors, elevators, and campus retail areas. She always seems pleasant, even while it takes great effort for her to accomplish tasks that we often take for granted.

I was quite excited when she entered my classroom at the beginning of one semester and took her place among the other students enrolled in this mandatory course. All that I observed about her from a distance proved accurate after getting to know her as a student. She was always on time, never late with an assignment, and one of the most eager participants in class discussions. I asked her outside of class, "What made you want to come here?" This was not an unusual question coming from me because I try to get all students to confront that question. However, her answer and the passion with which she answered caught me off-guard. "I see education as my way of standing up. I may never get out of this wheelchair, but I believe I can still walk just as tall as anybody," she said. Her achievement-oriented faith didn't end there. She plans to continue her education beyond undergraduate school and spoke of getting a master's and doctoral degree.

The evidence that drives her desire to achieve doesn't happen by accident. She's predisposed to believe in "next level" possibilities. She helped change my perspective on growth and achievement.

The most significant question is, "Will you have enough faith to move forward in the midst of major obstacles?" Achievement-oriented faith can help us overcome the worst of difficulties, whether we created them or not. The evidence of what we can become is resident in our faith.

Assumptions

Service is executed with the belief that spiritual maturity will occur in the process. Spiritual maturity increases one's service efficacy. Belief in the unseen fruit of personal growth or increased capacity validates the believer's efforts to attain the unseen. We develop tendencies to discount the power of subjective evidence. Yet, this is the essence of achievement-oriented faith. Objective evidence is the foundation of deductive reasoning and empirical science. We have been so indoctrinated to seek objective reality that we ignore the legitimacy and power of subjective evidence.

Faith stands as the only necessary evidence of subjective reality. Those who accept subjective reality do so under certain assumptions. For example, I believe if I study I'll become more knowledgeable; if I engage in spiritual disciplines, my relationship with God will improve; if I tithe, the windows of heaven will open. All of these assertions are accepted as truth by inductive, subjective reasoning. The conclusions can only be accepted by faith, for they absolutely defy objective analysis. Such subjective conclusions are the building blocks of achievement-oriented faith.

Growth occurs when evidential faith combines with ever-evolving, emerging service that seeks to do more, accomplish more, and provide more. For example,

> *Growth occurs when evidential faith combines with ever-evolving, emerging service that seeks to do more, accomplish more, and provide more.*

there are numerous ways to approach ministry team development. Organization development literature is replete with intervention models designed to encourage effective team relationships. Team building, role analysis, and team learning are just a few of the "buzz words" used to describe the multitude of interventions used to help teams become more efficient. Interventions that center on achievement-oriented faith are certainly worthy of consideration as models for team development.

Ministry team effectiveness is built on trust, interdependence, and respect. Achievement-oriented interventions place an emphasis on the utility of faith when facilitating individual and collective growth. Faith increases are viewed as directly proportional to improvement in a person's relationship with God. Service becomes more effective through personal submission and collective participation in service endeavors. Trust, interdependency, and respect promote healthy growth when supported by faith. The assumption is that faith is the ingredient that enables trust, interdependence, and respect to survive.

Members of ministry teams usually assume that everyone's trust is in the same place, in God. That's not to say that ministry team members don't need to trust each other. That's part of effective interdependency. However, achievement-oriented faith is placed in the Someone whom everyone assumes is the unseen group member. All members must perceive the unseen member, God, as the repository for ultimate trust. Some may argue that this breaks the rules of effective team development, contending that, "Any attempts to place trust in an unseen member is really a veiled attempt at avoidance, and that real issues are never effectively addressed." The truth is that effective internal team trust, interdependency, and respect can occur only when faith is operative. True interdependency occurs when vulnerability to other team members is accepted. True respect emerges when the value of others is acknowledged, despite their inefficiencies. Such obstacles are best overcome when there's an unwavering belief in the team's ability to achieve. Faith that focuses on continuous improvement, perpetual growth, increased effectiveness, and other growth ideals will enable the team to accept its vulnerabilities and bring about the type of freedom that heals ministry team ineffectiveness.

Common Experiences

Achievement-oriented servants find personal gratification in the growth experience. Their desires are centered on growth indicators and the extent to which advancement can be realized. The experience of one faith-style is sometimes best illuminated when contrasted with another faith-style. In this case, we gain a deeper understanding of the unique experiences of achievement-oriented servants by examining their experiences when they interact with those who have vision-oriented faith. They bring two very different perspectives to an encounter.

Consider this scenario: The ministry team has been given an assignment to explore the requirements for developing a vehicle donation program. The assignment requires a great deal of research. Internal revenue guidelines must be reviewed, and details of how the ministry will receive notifications from prospective donors require consideration. Agreements have to be developed with towing, storage, and salvage companies. As straightforward as the assignment may seem, difficulties may arise when approached from an achievement-oriented faith perspective, as opposed to a vision-oriented faith-style.

The primary objective of the assignment is for the ministry to raise funds by accepting donated vehicles. The objective is clearly financial, which may cause frustration for the achievement-oriented person. Achievement-oriented people view learning and spiritual growth as most essential. This doesn't mean that the two objectives are incompatible. People can certainly grow spiritually while pursuing financial goals. The difficulty occurs when individual priorities begin to conflict. If there's a choice of delaying the realization of the financial objective in the interest of gathering information, which may not be essential for program operation, achievement-oriented servants may choose to gather the information, causing purpose-driven servants to complain about unnecessary delays.

Neither approach is incorrect. It's a noble idea to gather as much information as possible, even if there's no immediate application. The purposeful notion of attaining the financial objective as soon as possible is also a good idea. The dilemma comes down to a matter of perspective. Achievement-oriented faith is recognized by the setting of measurable goals, not end points. Vision-oriented faith, or the purpose faith-style, is predicated on attaining an end. As far as the achievement-oriented servants are concerned, attaining one benchmark just means that it's time to move on to the next.

Their tendency to focus on growth and process instead of on purpose and content can lead to frustration for many achievement-oriented people. They must learn to bring closure to events, rather than having them evolve into a perpetual opportunity to learn. Most situations have an objective that must be fulfilled in order to measure progress. There's a time when the student has to graduate and apply some of the acquired knowledge. Growth and learning without application doesn't assist others. The more we're able to grow and apply our new capabilities, the more effectively we will serve.

Personality Traits

A strong desire to achieve particular objectives is referred to as *ambition*. There's no shortage of ambitious people in the world. We all know people who awake early and stay up late to accomplish what they deem important. Their behavior is either admired or disliked. We sometimes gravitate to people we perceive as ambitious because of admiration of their achievements, or we avoid them because their ambition seems misguided and unconscionably excessive.

In the context of achievement-oriented faith, ambitious personality takes on distinct characteristics. Ambitions are centered on achieving objectives consistent with God's desires. If people believe their actions will further God's plans, they display unwavering determination to make progress. Those who display such ambitions usually engage in many simultaneous activities to facilitate their progress. This is part of their signature behavior that defines the personality of achievement-oriented servants.

While it's not uncommon for achievement-oriented servants to possess simultaneous ambitions, it's true that their ambitions change. The only constant is that God's will remains the standard for ambitions. For instance, the aim this year may be to start a lunchtime Bible study. The objective five years from now may be to complete discipleship training. Ambitions change regularly, but the focus remains the same. This isn't to suggest that ambitions don't ever become misguided and self-centered. However, achievement-oriented faith has a way of realigning misguided ambitions with the mission, vision, goals, and objectives of ministry. Achievement-oriented faith leads people to take initiative. It's difficult to wait on others when growth opportunities are presented. Initiative is the order of the day when advancement is at stake. I recently observed a ministry situation in which this personality trait came very close to stalling an important project. Many of the leaders struggled with how to approach a person who seemed constantly to take action too far ahead of the other team members. The person's work was always superior in quality. Tasks were usually completed ahead of schedule and in great detail. However, when the ministry servant felt that progress was too slow, he took unauthorized liberties. The motives were pure, but the methods left a great deal to be desired. The dilemma was expressed in a question by one of the leaders: "How do we address his inappropriate behavior without killing his ambition?" A series of interventions were identified, including coaching, mediation, and feedback to make sure the intended message was not misunderstood, and the truth expressed in love.

Achievement-oriented servants may seem to have a single-minded focus that pursues growth at the expense of everything else, but this isn't necessarily true, for they make positive contributions to any ministry team. They may even prove to be quite flexible as long as progress is being made. They have a great deal of tolerance for uncertainty because growth is constantly requiring them to go into unfamiliar territory. All things considered, we would be less productive without achievement-oriented faith, which insures we will make increasingly powerful contributions to ministry and the mission of the church (see Table 7, "Achievement-Oriented Personality Traits and Conditional Factors").

Table 7
**Achievement-Oriented Personality Traits
and Conditional Factors**

PERSONALITY TRAIT	ENVIRONMENT	
	Simple	**Complex**
Ambitious	Style Contradiction	Style Consistency
Initiative		
Flexible		

Strengths

Charles Franklin Kettering (1876-1958), well-known U.S. engineer and inventor, once said, "The future can be anything we want it to be, providing we have the faith and that we realize that peace, no less than war, requires blood and sweat and tears." His remark perfectly describes the mindset that's the strength of the achievement-oriented faith-style. Growth suggests that the future is a state that exceeds the present in positive ways. Faith is the catalyst enabling us to actively pursue that future. Achievement-oriented servants possess a willingness to work and serve in a manner facilitating a positive future.

The strength of this faith-style lies in the ability to step beyond obstacles in the interest of an improved future.

The strength of this faith-style lies in the ability to step beyond obstacles in the interest of an improved future. The drive for growth is such that even obstacles are transformed into growth instruments. The commentary regarding obstacles doesn't deal with how the obstacle stopped progress. Instead, it focuses on the growth that occurred as a result of encountering the obstacle. The ability to view obstacles as growth opportunities enables achievement-oriented servants not to become immobilized, sacrificing important advancements.

Think of the implications of this positive aspect of achievement-oriented faith for service in ministry. Fewer ministry projects would be prematurely abandoned if obstacles were perceived as growth opportunities. The ministry would automatically be thrust into a mode of continuous improvement. People who bring this perspective to ministry teams can help lift teams beyond what appears to be self-imposed failures. When obstacles or mistakes are seen as self-imposed, they can be detrimental to the team's collective psyche. Obstacles are negative only when we fail to believe, learn, and grow from the experience.

Limitations

Like all others, the achievement-oriented faith-style has limitations. These may be overcome, but must be taken into consideration in order to achieve a more comprehensive understanding of the style. Achievement-oriented believers are often criticized for lack of focus on goals. Different benchmarks are utilized to indicate progress when growth is the primary goal.

Relationships may suffer because others have a different opinion about what constitutes progress. The pursuit of growth in the absence of objective evidence can be a nebulous exercise. Others who look for more concrete indicators of progress may become frustrated with what appears to be preparation in the absence of real results. Achievement-oriented servants can assist in overcoming such problems by communicating clearly about where and how their contributions may make the most significant impact. Everyone wants to achieve; there may simply be disagreement about how to make it happen.

Ministries and ministry projects are subject to life cycles, as are other organizations and ventures. As ministries progress, various stages of growth can bring about particular problems. Achievement-oriented faith tends to lead to blind advancement along the growth curve, failing to consider the particular pitfalls that are associated with various stages of growth. Growth is positive when it's understood and managed. Faith that's in this motif helps to energize ministry efforts effectively applied.

Summary

Achievement-oriented faith is based on the evidence of the unseen. Achievement is pursued despite the absence of objective evidence that anything will occur. Service is ever emerging when servants put achievement-oriented faith into action. Spiritual maturity is the aim of those who possess achievement-oriented faith. It's achieved through the power of a person's acceptance of subjective evidence, leading to truth.

Ministry teams can benefit tremendously when achievement-oriented faith is operative. The team is able to utilize achievement-orientated faith to move beyond obstacles and help to incorporate past learnings into future endeavors. Obstacles are transformed into learning opportunities, contributing to the growth of the individual servant or the team. A willingness to go into unchartered experiences contributes to growth.

I again emphasize the importance of balance on ministry teams. All faith-styles are necessary, and style diversity is a tremendous asset to any ministry effort. People must discover their individual styles and think about the implications for serving with people who possess different styles. Proverbs 4:7 tells us, "Wisdom is supreme; therefore get wisdom: Though it cost all you have, get understanding." Understanding the various faith-style orientations facilitates a greater level of performance in ministry. It also generates freedom to serve, as the understanding strengthens relationships inside and outside of ministry groups. The Servant Resource Faith-Style Model provides an excellent framework to begin the process of understanding.

Discussion Guide

1. List three personal achievements that you would like to accomplish which require the most faith.

2. Develop a strategy for overcoming the tendency to focus on preparation rather than application.

3. Distinguish between and state the benefits of quantitative and qualitative growth.

4. What are the advantages that the achievement-oriented faith-style contributes to ministry teams?

5. Identify some of the potential disadvantages that the achievement-oriented faith-style contributes to ministry teams.

Serving God with style —

— Just styles —

1. Who am I
2. What is my role?
3. Who are we?
4. Who are we becoming?
5. How do we get to where we're going

The Last Word
on Faith-Styles

The title of this chapter is somewhat of a misnomer. I'm not näive or arrogant enough to believe that I'll actually have the final word on faith-styles. My prayer is that the introduction of this concept will stimulate dialogue that continues long beyond my direct involvement. The basic goal of this book is to assist all who love God and who work to advance ministry answer five basic questions relating to faith and service: (1) Who am I? (2) What is my role? (3) Who are we? (4) Who are we becoming? and (5) How do we get where we're going? The unleashing of servant potential is resident in the answers to these questions. The Servant Resource Faith-Style Model and the Servant Resource Faith-Style Inventory are simply tools that will facilitate the journey.

A personal, collective, and continual quest to answer each question is an important ingredient for individual spiritual growth and congregational well-being. We personally answer the questions so that we'll have a grasp of our uniqueness and value in the kingdom of God. We answer the questions collectively in order to build a platform for meaningful relationships with others. And because we don't live and serve in a static world, the questions must be addressed continually so that we remain relevant in our understanding.

The importance of these questions shouldn't be underestimated. It's wonderful to discover information about yourself, but the information will fall short of its potential value if there is no framework for application. The questions will help to crystallize the faith-style concept and provide even more ideas for application. For that reason, I'm devoting the remaining pages of this final chapter to sharing insights related to each one of them. Identity, role, relationship, and strategy are the essential elements for transforming style into congregational strength.

Who Am I?

I've always been intrigued by the television dramas that feature episodes involving amnesia. First, let me say that I realize that art is imitating real life and that amnesia is a condition with which many struggle. However, in the safety of fictional television, it does set the stage for great drama. The scenarios usually unfold like this. One of the main characters experiences a trauma, physical or psychological in nature. A bump on the head often does the trick. Or it could be the witnessing of an event that's so emotionally traumatic that it causes a portion of the character's memory to take leave. Then we are treated to a series of experiences in which the character wrestles with the inability to establish identity that means anything to him or her, or to establish points of reference that will give meaning. Then, the condition is reversed by another bump on the head or an emotional event that stimulates memory paths and reservoirs.

I know that I'm not alone when I say I'm intrigued by such drama. The reason this theme is so recurring in movies and television is that writers and producers know it attracts viewers. Industry decision-makers know that personal identity is so essential to our being that the mere thought of losing all points of personal reference brings us to the edge of our seats. But there are deeper implications here. It's certainly good to have knowledge of what could be considered superficial identifiers—name, rank, and serial number—but what about

Deep spiritual identity enables us to navigate confidently the difficulties of the human experience so that we can move beyond our focus on self and to see the blessing in serving others.

being able to answer the question regarding our inner identity? Deep spiritual identity enables us to navigate confidently the difficulties of the human experience so that we can move beyond our focus on self and to see the blessing in serving others. This is the crossroads where a keen awareness of personal spiritual identity is transformed into the ability to render tireless service, and servant potential is attained.

Congregational leaders have the responsibility of helping individual members regain their sense of identity. Just like the players in a made-for-television drama, spiritual identities are sometimes forgotten because of traumatic experience or some other undetectable cause. However, we all benefit when people find themselves spiritually. Their heightened sense of identity liberates them to become more effective contributors to the mission of the church. I've too often witnessed the deflated sense of identity that people experience because of church events that challenge their point of view. A challenged point of view can be a very traumatic experience for some of us, and the ensuing behavior can sometimes lead people to believe that they've forgotten who they are, who God created them to be, and what their identity in Christ says about them.

Faith-styles are one piece of the personal-identity puzzle. I'm not sure that we ever get the complete picture. The book of our lives is still being written. The best we can do is rediscover ourselves in the context of each new chapter. Our dominant faith-style will tend to remain the same, but the manner in which the style is expressed will change as the situations change.

Don't hesitate to retake the inventory or review your results as time passes. Some of your most liberating revelations will occur the second, third, and fourth times you analyze your style. It will also be helpful to cross-examine your style against the perceptions of others because of our tendency to develop images as we think or wish them to be. It's not that we're allowing others to define us, but their perceptions of us can certainly provide valuable clues about the identity we project, as opposed to the one that actually exists.

Our concept of service says a great deal about our true identity. When God shapes our identity, we begin to realize that we have a unique role to play in God's plan and purpose.

Where Do I Fit?

One of the most perplexing, and even frustrating, questions for people involved in congregational or any other group activities is, "Where do I fit?" The question emerges from other underlying ideas about who we are, what value we bring, and how we are accepted by others. Many of us have probably witnessed the difficulties that can arise when a person doesn't understand her or his role. Undefined or misunderstood roles create a fertile environment for negative conflict. I hope that the preceding chapters have helped you to get a better grasp on "where you fit." If you have a clearer perspective about who and where God uniquely created you to be, you've had a liberating experience.

There's nothing more disheartening than watching people attempt to serve outside of their niche. It's not just frustrating for the individual. Their misalignment can give birth to a myriad of problems for the entire group. Ministry team members should answer this question and become comfortable with the answer before engaging in any ministry assignment. This isn't to say that one's role will always be defined the same way. But understanding where we fit enables us to enter ministry assignments with a clearer sense of purpose and our unique contribution. Understanding one's unique faith-style is just one additional tool that will enable ministry servants to say with more confidence, "I understand how and where I fit in."

I've become even more aware in recent months of the importance of understanding one's niche. The ministry in which I serve (as well as a few others for whom I serve in a consulting capacity) are experiencing tremendous growth. They are in the process of expanding their staffs. One of the greatest concerns pastors have isn't about finding the most technically qualified candidate. They are equally, if not more, concerned with whether they will find a candidate who is a good fit. Will they fit in with our existing staff? Will they be able to adapt to the culture? How will their interjection of their role fit in with the shifting roles and responsibilities of others? The bottom-line question for the new member is, "Where and how will I fit?"

Those who recognize the extreme importance of this question are probably aware of the importance because of an experience in which the question of "fit" was not considered. What happens when we are left to find our fit by trial and error? A situation is created in which we have to "feel our way around in the dark." Normal adjustments be-come much more

Helping congregational members find their niche helps build strong congregational community, a sense of "we're all in this together."

difficult because the issue of belonging has not been rectified. Finding your niche will provide a sense of belonging. But it's much more difficult to find your niche if the invitation to search is never expressed or facilitated. When the issue of "fit" is not raised, we find ourselves in situations that are uncomfortable for everyone involved. We are then left with the awkward task of having to communicate the absence of compatibility without devaluing the people involved. We then run the risk of having "this is not your niche" interpreted as "there is no place for you." This is a risk that is too high to accept when dealing with servant potential.

The importance of such questions further illuminates the significance of tools such as the Servant Resource Faith-Style Inventory. Helping people find their niche will assist in our efforts to build strong ministries and productive congregations. There is a place for everyone. We all have a contribution to make. Helping congregational members find their niche helps build strong congregational community, a sense of "we're all in this together." We may be different. We may see the world from slightly different perspectives. But we have a common purpose in Christ that is expansive enough to accommodate everyone who desires to contribute. Our place in the service to our Lord is secure, all we have to do is find it and help others find theirs.

Who Are We?

When we come together in service, bringing our individual faith-styles, a collective identity emerges. We often hear this identity referred to by different terms, such as *church culture.* Nevertheless, congregations and groups have identities that are as unique as the personalities of individuals. Awareness of our collective identity is as important as our awareness of our individual identity. Understanding who we are is important for several reasons.

Our collective identity establishes norms by which new members come to understand what membership means. As we bring people into the body of faith, we also have to make sure we introduce them to our uniqueness. Who hasn't witnessed the difficulties new members experience as they seek to become integrated into church life? They join a congregation based on a perceived need, rather than a true understanding of the collective identity and characteristics of the ministry. They visit on Sunday morning, enjoy the worship, are inspired by the message, but really don't know the collective character of the ministry. Truthfully, the only way to gain this kind of intimate knowledge is by purposefully observing and gathering information about the full range of church activities. Even beyond the general sharing of information about the mission and vision of the church, tools are needed that can assist congregations in gaining a greater understanding of their evolving collective identity or culture.

An understanding of the collective identity not only helps to establish norms by which members are more effectively integrated into church life; it provides a coherent view for those who may be observing from outside the ministry. There are congregations that seem to be able to be all things to all people at all times. Those that are able to accomplish this feat are extremely rare. Of course the primary purpose of any Christian congregation is to work for the fulfillment of the Great Commission. Yet, every church has a unique way of approaching the task. Even within denominational constructs, every ministry has its own special way. People observing from the outside get a much clearer, more accurate picture when those on the inside know themselves. Many factors, such as pastoral leadership, board composition, geographic location, and many other circumstances, may contribute to their uniqueness. But failure to foster internal awareness of the collective make-up of the ministry can create inconsistencies that become observable by those we seek to attract.

Although faith-styles are most often discussed in terms of individual spiritual growth and awareness, we should never underestimate their value in our efforts to collectively grasp "who we are." This is true on a ministry-group level and a ministry-wide level. Knowledge of ministry-wide faith-style characteristics provides information that will enable ministry participants to understand and better articulate "who we are." Just as Rick Warren's popular book *The Purpose-Driven Church* describes ministry-wide characteristics that establish a set of defining criteria for quality and purpose, a church finds value in establishing criteria and identity around behaviors as they relate to faith and service.[1] Situations may arise in which the need to answer the question, "Who Are We?" becomes obviously more important. Two scenarios readily come to mind: *(a)* during times of significant change, such as growth, and *(b)* during times of extreme difficulty, such as conflict. Difficulties have a way of causing us to lose our collective sense of identity. It is as if we all suddenly want to be somebody else, so everybody tries to create a new image that becomes one of disharmony. And times of rapid change make the old adage "We aren't what we used to be" much more a reality than we sometimes care to accept. Regardless of the situation, our ability to understand ourselves collectively is important to our ability to develop and deliver effective ministry.

Who Are We Becoming?

Rather than saying, "We aren't what we used to be," it's more accurate to say, "We aren't who we used to be." The collective faith-style profile, the summation of individual faith-styles within a group or ministry, is ever changing. It's continuously evolving throughout the life of the ministry. That's why it's important to engage in continuous monitoring of a congregation's collective profile, working to develop an understanding of "who we are becoming."

The congregation where I currently serve has experienced tremendous growth over the past several years. The evolution of our collective identity has been tremendously accelerated, and there is no reason at this point to anticipate a deceleration in growth. One retrospective observation is that no stages along the journey have been identical. There are those who have been members through the entire experience. There are also those who are no longer with us. And even those who have been with us through every transition have evolved and changed as individuals. This doesn't necessarily mean that their dominant faith-styles have changed. But it does suggest that their awareness may have increased

The fact that we continuously evolve individually and congregationally suggests that we must always have an eye on "who we are becoming" collectively.

and they may have improved their ability to work with others who have different styles.

The fact that we continuously evolve individually and congregationally suggests that we must always have an eye on "who we are becoming" collectively. Looking ahead is not necessarily for the purpose of attempting to shape every detail of our future. To do so would be to deny that God has any say in the matter. The real purpose for understanding the collective faith-style mix is to have a greater awareness of where God is taking us so that we can effectively and cooperatively move in the same direction.

How Do We Get Where We're Going?

In my studies of Western and Eastern organizational cultures, I've become aware of a fundamental truth regarding the way in which each culture tends to approach tasks. In Eastern cultures, it takes a relatively long time to make organizational decisions. Extended time may be necessary because relationship is so highly regarded. The well-being of the collective takes precedence over individual rights. Consensus building is of primary importance. If there is no consensus, the decision will not be finalized. Decision making is a slow process, but implementation occurs relatively quickly. Westerners are exactly the opposite. The emphasis on individual rights and positional power and authority makes decision making a quick process. Consequently, implementation is relatively slow, sometimes because buy-in did not exist.

I believe that this reality is also present in our ministry organizations. Implementation can be a slow, arduous process. Many valuable ministry programs fall victim to this phenomenon. "Our wonderful, esteemed Pastor made the decision," we hear, "and rightfully so." He or she is the called shepherd of God. However, his or her decision may have been made without considering the issues of buy-in and implementation. That's why a more appropriate title for this section may be "How Do We Get Started?" It's wonderful to raise awareness about faith-styles. The question after the awareness point becomes, "Then what do we do?"

First, forums for dialogue must be established. People will be able to gain wonderful insight into personal behavioral patterns, aspects of faith and service that will enable them to become more focused in ministry efforts. Conversation about this wonderfully new insight must be more than incidental conversation at the church picnic. There should be scheduled structure events during which individuals have an opportunity to share, discover new meaning, and discuss application for their new insight regarding their place in service activities. Servants must strategize about how the information will alter their individual approach to service.

There must also be opportunities for groups and teams to dialogue regarding both ongoing and ad hoc ministry programs. Ministry teams who regularly serve together will be strengthened by their new insight regarding faith-styles. Faith-style discussions can become a regular part of ministry team meetings. Facilitator roles can be alternated among members so that all members experience the discussion from the perspective of having to lead faith-style discussions. Even groups that have a limited assignment can benefit from faith-style discussions. The dialogue will tend to minimize the time ministry teams spend in unproductive stages, accelerating their progress toward optimum performance.

Planning opportunities for dialogue concerning personal faith-style strategies and team faith-style strategies are tremendously important. However, it is also important to utilize different strategic interventions to integrate the faith-style concept and help it to permeate the ministry. Some sessions will be simply for strategy development, others will be for ministry team building, some will be purely instructional, and others will be consultative. Regardless of

Serving God with Style

the type of intervention, the overall ministry will benefit from a comprehensive faith-style approach.

I pray that you have been blessed by the contents of this book. It is not meant to be the answer to all of your faith- and service-related problems. However, I believe that combined with faith, it will give you a fresh approach, one that you've not seen or utilized before. That freshness born out of the creative power of God's Spirit is like the "living water" that Jesus spoke of in the fourth chapter of John. He told the Samaritan woman, "Everyone who drinks this water will be thirsty again, but whoever drinks the water I give him will never thirst. Indeed, the water I give him will become in him a spring of water welling up to eternal life" (John 4:13-14). May you be renewed, revived, and encouraged as faith-styles become part of your approach to eternity.

The Servant Resource Faith-Style Inventory

Instructions: For each of the following phrases in italics, rank the four statements in the order that completes the phrase to your best satisfaction. Give your most favored statement a rank of 4, your next favored a rank of 3, your next 2, and your least favored statement a rank of 1. Place your ranking for each on the line to the right of the statement.

1. *In planning, God leads me to*
   - establish goals while remaining hopeful to exceed them   ____(a)
   - see the big picture before my colleagues   ____(b)
   - work on implementation rather than strategy   ____(c)
   - encourage others by generating excitement   ____(d)

2. *God enables people to do their best*
   - when they believe they're fulfilling their potential and reaching their capacity as human beings   ____(e)
   - when they understand the underlying reasons for their actions   ____(f)
   - when there's enough activity to generate results   ____(g)
   - when they spend time in reflection and prayer   ____(h)

3. *A faith-oriented view of service emphasizes*
   - the personal development and advancement   ____(a)
   - the realization of a desired result   ____(b)
   - action-oriented, specific goals   ____(c)
   - the generation of better materials and goods using imaginative methods   ____(d)

4. *Most of what God enables people to produce*
   - encourages them to strive for higher productivity   ____(e)
   - is done from a desire to achieve the "big picture"   ____ (f)
   - is possible because of a focus on "getting things done"   ____(g)
   - is the result of divine revelation   ____(h)

5. *Decisions about one's service*
   - will lead to an increase in knowledge and results   ____(a)
   - are intentional and deliberate   ____(b)
   - can lead to opportunities to serve   ____(c)
   - are often made without a great deal of premeditation   ____(d)

6. *Faith-based servants*
   - seek greater challenges   ____(e)
   - work toward long-term goals   ____(f)
   - focus on starting new programs   ____(g)
   - often introduce new techniques   ____(h)

7. *Lack of faith is most evident when one*
   - neglects new opportunities   ____(a)
   - loses sight of goals   ____(b)
   - is inactive   ____(c)
   - appears to have no energy to perform   ____(d)

8. *It's easier to exercise faith when there are*
   - opportunities for advancement   ____(e)
   - well-written vision statements   ____(f)
   - well-defined goals, objectives, and action items   ____(g)
   - dynamic leaders involved   ____(h)

9. *When I'm uncertain about decisions related to my service*
   - the opportunity to learn is more important than making
     the correct decision   ____(a)
   - I refer to the mission or objective   ____(b)
   - I tend to start working before receiving complete
     instructions   ____(c)
   - I look to people I respect to help motivate me   ____(d)

10. *When serving*
- I love to admire the final product ____(e)
- I plan projects in phases with an ultimate goal in mind ____(f)
- I initiate multiple projects at the same time ____(g)
- I'm comfortable improvising ____(h)

11. *When faith is applied in service, it's most beneficial for*
- advancing to the next level of service ____(a)
- advancing the overall cause of the group or organization ____(b)
- gaining clarity about the specific activities to be done ____(c)
- motivating potential servants ____(d)

12. *When difficulties arise while serving*
- they become opportunities to learn ____(e)
- they're part of a divine plan ____(f)
- I believe they can be overcome by working harder ____(g)
- spiritual renewal is the key to success ____(h)

13. *Faith-based performance is demonstrated best*
- by one's ability to take actions of increasing difficulty ____(a)
- by one's ability to understand how the job fits the overall strategy ____(b)
- when results are observable ____(c)
- when the product is the result of spontaneous action ____(d)

14. *Faith-based servants are most satisfied when*
- they get recognition for good works ____(e)
- they believe in the program objectives ____(f)
- they have a clear agenda ____(g)
- they're allowed to "dream" ____(h)

15. *If your faith is tried in a service situation, it helps to*
- seek opportunities to initiate new activities ____(a)
- review the aim of the program ____(b)
- review goals for each service worker ____(c)
- draw upon internal strength and fortitude ____(d)

Interpreting the Servant Resource Faith-Style Inventory

Instructions: Sum all the numbers you placed in the "a" and "e" boxes in the Faith-Style Inventory. Place the total on the "a + e" line in the figure below. This is your growth orientation score. Repeat this process for the following totals: "d + h"; "b + f"; and "c + g." Service is viewed as an activity that requires intense planning and incremental implementation of interpretive material as it applies to your profile (see Figure 3).

Figure 3
Faith-Style Inventory Interpretation

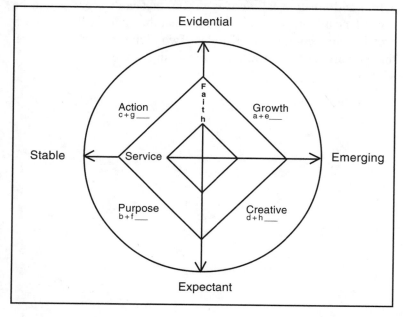

Evidential: Faith is evidenced by objective activity that one believes will lead to progress.

Expectant: Faith is observed in spontaneous expressions of hope that facilitate progress toward a desired objective.

Stable: Service is an activity that requires intense planning and incremental implementation.

Emerging: Service is the result of unpredictable needs that require situational approaches.

Higher scores indicate dominant faith-styles. Refer to the "Elements of Servant Resource Faith-Style" for further interpretation (appendix 3).

High scores may occur in two seemingly contradictory styles. Styles that are opposites represent two ends of a continuum. If your score is high on one end (e.g. creative faith) and low on the other (e.g. action faith), your score would be illustrated on the continuum as a point on the extreme end of creative faith. A high score on both action and creative faith-styles means that your score would be toward the middle of the continuum, near the dividing line between creative and action-oriented styles. Two high scores simply mean that you are more comfortably able to shift styles.

Elements of Servant Resource Faith-Style

FAITH ORIENTATION	ACTION Responsibility Orientation	PURPOSE Vision Orientation	CREATIVE Experiment Orientation	GROWTH Achievement Orientation
ASSUMPTIONS	• Faith is demonstrated by one's uncompromising commitment to action • Faith without "specific" works is dead. The care that's taken to initiate action is an indicator of a person's belief that the activity can be accomplished	• Properly applied faith will lead to the realization of a specific vision • Visions are likely to be achieved in a progressive manner just as they were originally conceived • Faith can be used as a tool to achieve exact, distinct objectives with surgical precision	• We're created in God's image; therefore, we have re-creative capacity that's generated from our reliance on God • Faith can bring what didn't previously exist into being • The ability to create is directly related to one's ability to believe	• Service is executed with the belief that spiritual maturity will occur in the process • As spiritual maturity increases, one's service efficacy increases • The relationship between effort and achievement is directly proportional in the strengthening of one's faith
COMMON EXPERIENCES	• Feels like the "activity police" when serving with others • Usually prefers to serve alone • Has the reputation as a "get-the-job-done" person • Good at showing measurable results	• Sees the "big pictures" before others • May appear or tend to act prematurely • People tend to listen and follow • May experience feelings of being out-of-control in periods of accelerating change	• May appear to be "over-the-edge" • Will act without concern for resources • Often "out-on-a-limb" with God • Criticized by more conventional thinkers • More concerned with the journey than the results	• Financial gratification is delayed for opportunities of intellectual and spiritual growth • Personal benchmarks are established, but not end points • Tendency to frequently go beyond recognized capabilities

PERSONALITY TRAITS	ACTION	PURPOSE	CREATIVE	GROWTH
	• Reliable • Accountable • Goal-oriented • Results-conscious	• Focused • Intentional • Prudent • Confident	• Innovative • Calculated risk-taker • Free-spirited • Unconventional	• Ambitious • Initiative • Flexible
STRENGTHS	• Able to stay on track • Accomplishes activity in an objectively measurable manner	• Maintains sight of the "why" of actions taken • Able to avoid diversions • Brings surety to a group	• Copes well with change and uncertainty • Ability to innovate and generate new ideas	• Future-oriented • Able to move beyond obstacles
LIMITATIONS	• Not adaptable to change • Limits creative capacity • Frustrated when attention is diverted from specific activities	• Restricts the movement of God • Leaves little room for change • Easily frustrated by the lack of vision of others	• May appear to lack direction and purpose • Lacks attention to time constraints • A tendency to not adhere to structure and order	• Lacks focused goals • Relationships may suffer • Perpetual state of preparation may never lead to application

NOTES

Introduction

1. Here and throughout this book, the biblical translation used, unless otherwise noted, will be the *New International Version* (International Bible Society, 1984). The *King James Version* will be identified as KJV, the *New Revised Standard Version* as NRSV.

2. The Servant Resource Faith-Style Inventory is for the purpose of facilitating discussion in and among ministry teams. It has not been subjected to validity and reliability testing that would qualify it as a decision-making tool. The structure was adapted from the Training Style Inventory by Richard Brostrom, *The 1979 Annual Handbook for Group Facilitators* (San Diego: Pfeiffer & Company, 1979). For examples of other style inventories see Maurice Lorr, *Interpersonal Style Inventory* (Los Angeles: Western Psychological Services, 1986); David A. Kolb, *Learning Style Inventory* (Boston: McBer and Co., 1985); and Marshall Sashkin, *Conflict Style Inventory* (Amherst: Human Resource Development Press, 1995).

Chapter 1

1. From Biblesoft's *New Exhaustive Strong's Numbers and Concordance with Expanded Greek-Hebrew Dictionary* (Seattle: Biblesoft and International Bible Translators, Inc., 1994), adapted from Dr. James Strong's *Old Testament Hebrew/Chaldee and New Testament Greek Dictionaries*, first published in 1894.

2. Ibid.

Chapter 3
1. J. P. Chaplin, *Dictionary of Psychology* (New York: Dell Publishing, 1985).

Chapter 10
1. Gareth Morgan, *Images of Organization* (Thousand Oaks, Calif.: Sage Publishing, 1996), 47.

Conclusion
1. Rick Warren, *The Purpose-Driven Church* (Grand Rapids: Zondervan, 1995).

Faith Style Seminars
Unleashing Servant Potential

There's untapped potential in your congregation
just waiting to be released.

Yes! I am interested in bringing *Faith Style Seminars*
to my ministry.

Seminar Format (Check One):
- ❑ One-Hour Introduction
- ❑ Three-Hour (Half-Day) Seminar
- ❑ Six-Hour (One-Day) Seminar

Name_____

Ministry Organization_____

Ministry Position _____

Address _____

_____

Telephone _____

Fax _____

Email _____

Call 410-945-7832 or 1-866-ASK-CCE7 (275-2237) toll free
or
Fax the completed form to 410-945-0541
Email to

Center for Church Empowerment Inc.
Attention: Faith Style Seminars
4501 ½ Old Frederick Road
Baltimore, Maryland 21229

Welcome to the work of Alban Institute...
the leading publisher and congregational resource organization for clergy and laity today.

Your purchase of this book means you have an interest in the kinds of information, research, consulting, networking opportunities and educational seminars that Alban Institute produces and provides. We are a non-denominational, non-profit 25-year-old membership organization dedicated to providing practical and useful support to religious congregations and those who participate in and lead them.

Alban is acknowledged as a pioneer in learning and teaching on *Conflict Management *Faith and Money *Congregational Growth and Change *Leadership Development *Mission and Planning *Clergy Recruitment and Training *Clergy Support, Self-Care and Transition *Spirituality and Faith Development *Congregational Security.

Our membership is comprised of over 8,000 clergy, lay leaders, congregations and institutions who benefit from:
- ❖ 15% discount on hundreds of Alban books
- ❖ $50 per-course tuition discount on education seminars
- ❖ Subscription to *Congregations*, the Alban journal (a $30 value)
- ❖ Access to Alban research and (soon) the "Members-Only" archival section of our web site www.alban.org

For more information on Alban membership or to be added to our catalog mailing list, call 1-800-486-1318, ext.243 or return this form.

Name and Title: _____

Congregation/Organization: _____

Address: _____

City: _____ Tel.: _____

State: _____ Zip: _____ Email: _____

BKIN

The Alban Institute
Attn: Membership Dept.
7315 Wisconsin Avenue
Suite 1250 West
Bethesda, MD 20814-3211